THE MASTER ARCHITECT SERIES III

Alfredo De Vido

Selected and Current Works

THE MASTER ARCHITECT SERIES III

Alfredo De Vido

Selected and Current Works

First published in Australia in 1998 by
The Images Publishing Group Pty Ltd
ACN 059 734 431
6 Bastow Place, Mulgrave, Victoria, 3170
Telephone (61 3) 9561 5544 Facsimile (61 3) 9561 4860

National Library of Australia Cataloguing-in-Publication Data

De Vido, Alfredo, 1932–
Alfredo De Vido: selected and current works.

Bibliography.
Includes index.
ISBN 1 875498 76 1

1. De Vido, Alfredo, 1932– . 2. Architecture, Modern—20th
century—United States. 3. Architecture, American. 4. Architects
—United States. I. Title. (Series: Master architect series).

720.92

Edited by Stephen Dobney
Designed by The Graphic Image Studio Pty Ltd,
Mulgrave, Australia
Film by Scanagraphix Australia Pty Ltd
Printed in Hong Kong

Contents

9   Introduction
     The Architecture of Alfredo De Vido
     By Michael J. Crosbie

Work Places

18   Lee's Art Shop
20   Church's English Shoes
21   Berk of Burlington Arcade
22   Tess
24   Catherine Atzen Day Spa
26   Word of Mouth/Cafe Word of Mouth
32   Stuarts Restaurant
34   La Chausseria
36   J.J. Lally Chinese Art
38   Wig Shop
40   Troa Cho Boutique
42   Ranch 1 Fast Food Restaurant
44   Offices for Import Associates Inc.
45   Muir, Cornelius, Moore Office Renovation
46   70 East 10th Street, New York
48   Lobby Renovation, 108 East 16th Street
50   Architect's Office, 699 Madison Avenue
52   WebGenesis
54   Allendale Park Modular Industrial Buildings
57   Evidence Vehicle Facility
60   Silver Sands State Park

Gathering Places

64   Wolf Trap Farm Park
68   Mann Music Center
72   Brooklyn Academy of Music Renovation
74   Manhattan School of Music Renovation/Addition
77   Henry and Edsel Ford Auditorium Renovation
78   Queens Theatre in the Park
82   The Diller-Quaile School of Music
83   Stephen Gaynor School
84   The Allen-Stevenson School
86   Chapel of Mt St Dominic
90   Community Church of Astoria

Shelter

96   Moore House
100 Wirth House
103 Minton House
104 Sheehy House
106 Garraty House
108 Sametz House
110 West House
112 Wertheimer House
116 Farese House
118 Matthews House
121 Duffy House
122 De Vido House
127 Ross House
128 3 White Pine Road
130 1 White Pine Road
134 Hammer House
136 Built-for-Sale House
137 Goodman House
138 Fried House
140 Snow King Inn
145 Berkowitz Addition/Renovation
146 Yang House
147 McCombe House
148 Greenbriar
150 Leader House
152 Sara House
155 Kleinman House
156 New Preston House
158 Ferguson House
159 Boyle House
160 Aksen House
161 David Alan House
164 Vuolo House
166 Concept House
167 Gropp House
168 Morton House
170 Rothschild House
172 Butler/Schnur House, 10 White Pine Road
174 Frocht House
178 Kessler House
180 Wright House
182 The Royale
186 222 Columbia Heights
190 54 Willow Street
192 Jonathan's Landing
194 Apartment, 61 East 86 Street
198 Cohalan House
200 Staten Island House
204 McConomy Poolhouse, Garden, and Pavilions
209 Trosin House
210 Drake House
216 New Vernon House
218 Quinones/Bieganek House
221 Meadow Way House
222 House in Bridgehampton
224 Haidinger House
226 Rafferty House
227 Columbia County House
228 Megerle House
230 Moellentine House
231 Peters House
232 Turchin House
234 Senkirk House
236 Architect's House and Office, 412 East 85th Street

Furniture and Lighting

243 Furniture and Lighting

Firm Profile

249 Biography
250 Selected Awards
251 Selected Bibliography
252 Acknowledgments
253 Index

Introduction

Introduction

The Architecture of Alfredo De Vido

By Michael J. Crosbie

The architecture of Alfredo De Vido is not easy to categorize. Developing a recognizable, repeatable "signature style" has long been a strategy for architects who wish to market their designs as one would any art object. Indeed, rigidly predictable styles have been the bedrock of marketable art for ages. But this architect's approach to design springs from other values. An interest in formal experimentation pervades De Vido's work, as does a commitment to answering the design challenges at hand, regardless of the style.

For example, De Vido meets the need for an affordable structure by developing a modular design system that makes the contractor's job easier, with less waste, simpler working drawings, and faster construction. The buildings are laid out on a 10-foot module, with internal spaces broken down into multiples or divisions of 10. Another modular dimension governs all vertical locations for floors, doors, and windows. This system results in projects that are easier to build and reduces on-site mistakes without sacrificing unique design. And it dovetails with De Vido's interest in proportional order and composition.

Such practical, ingenious solutions also suggest the architect's background in design and construction while serving in the US Navy's "Seabees" (construction battalions), an experience which left him with an appreciation of the demands of the worksite. Many of De Vido's buildings, especially his houses, exude a craftsman's appreciation for the way in which structure and materials come together in celebratory expression. The material nature of architecture is just one of De Vido's influences. To borrow a distinction from the late Bill Turnbull (a classmate of De Vido's at Princeton), this architect is inspired by the "concrete and tangible" as opposed to the "abstract or metaphorical" —the qualities one finds in real sites, real clients, and real design problems. De Vido also points to his experiences in Japan and Scandinavia, and his own Italian ethnicity, as constituting a culturally rich architectural heritage on which to draw.

While De Vido's work is free from a monotonous trademark style for these reasons, there are a number of themes apparent in the projects presented in this book that cut across the architect's entire oeuvre. Five themes—Earth and Sun, The Sheltering Roof, Space at the Heart, Pure Geometries, and Respect for Context—emerge as generators of form. Some are found in combination in a number of buildings, while others are apparent in their purest form in individual works. There are no doubt other characteristics in De Vido's architecture, but these five themes emerge again and again as the seeds from which entire buildings grow.

Earth and Sun

The desire to express a building's connection to the natural world—particularly how it merges with the site and captures natural light—has long been a generating theme in architecture around the world. In De Vido's architecture, part of the intention is to conserve energy through the generous introduction of natural light. A good example of this design strategy is the Megerle House in North Castle, New York, in which De Vido takes a rectilinear form and fractures it with glazed walls oriented to the south to maximize solar exposure. The client's request for a garden room resulted in an indoor pool surrounded by greenery. Solar collectors heat the pool's water. This garden room is covered with a glass roof, with a stepped wall oriented to frame views of a nearby pond. Other spaces in the house collect around this sun-catching space.

Another approach is literally to link the building with the earth, as in the Cohalan House in Bayport, New York, in which a cubical form appears to grow from the bermed site surrounding it. In this case, the first floor was raised to avoid a high water table, and natural illumination from skylights brightens and warms the below-grade spaces. The house's natural wood siding merges with the green ground cover of the surrounding berms.

Undoubtedly one of De Vido's greatest works, the Moore House in Sharon, Connecticut (found on the cover of this monograph), appears to have literally grown from a gentle hillside, bringing earth and sun together with interiors of natural stone, wood, and concrete.

The house is linear, opening up along its entire south side to sunlight and views. The north side backs against the hill. The spaces here are punctuated with skylights, which wash the rough fieldstone walls with sunshine. The grass roof, treed courtyard, and site-grown oak beams all serve to blur the line at which the land ends and the house begins.

The Sheltering Roof

Gable roofs are universal symbols of home, with the power to evoke a sense of security. Several of De Vido's projects employ the sheltering roof as a form-giver, the over-arching symbol of protected refuge. In a series of built-for-sale houses in East Hampton, New York, expansive gable roofs dominate the designs, connecting in some cases with shed roofs to suggest "bent" gables. McKim, Mead & White's Low House of 1887 is an obvious precedent here, as is Robert Venturi's house for his mother, yet the form is timeless.

In another De Vido project, the Minton House in Copake, New York, the gable end of the house becomes a canvas upon which the architect arranges a series of square windows, revealing the spacious interiors. At night, with the windows aglow, the gable form is reiterated. The southeast side of the Minton House is occupied by a sunny deck, and the gable form appears again where two shed roofs meet at right angles.

The house at 1 White Pine Road employs gable forms as a device to manipulate the building's delicate scale. On the entry side, a small gable form meets the visitor at the front door, and is echoed to either side by larger gabled wings. On the opposite side of the house, the central gable enlarges to become a gracious loggia leading to a deck. Gable roofs are repeated on the house's ends and inside the large, two-story living room.

De Vido's use of the gable to communicate a sense of welcome and warmth is not restricted to residences. In his renovation and addition design for the Community Church of Astoria, New York, the gable form becomes a symbol of a house of worship— a veritable religious billboard in this urban neighborhood.

Space at the Heart

Dynamic, soaring space is at the heart of Modern architecture, and one finds it at the heart of many of De Vido's designs. For this architect, it becomes architecture's vital organ, to which every other space in the building is subservient. It is also the nesting place, where one collects and restores the sense of dwelling. So critical an element is this space at the heart, that it appears early and often in De Vido's work, most notably in his own house in East Hampton, New York, which he started building 30 years ago and continues to embellish to this day. In his own house, the central, two-story space becomes the axis around which the rest of the spaces rotate, filled with sunlight and the raw tectonics of rough-hewn, post-and-beam construction. In the Snow King Inn at Jackson, Wyoming, the central space is again defined by muscular structure in the form of heavy wood trusses above, and is marked with a rustic stone fireplace that reaches up through the volume.

A slightly different approach is found in the house in New Vernon, New Jersey, where the central space of the family room is defined not by structure and natural materials, but by smooth, sculptural surfaces. De Vido employs stepped forms to bounce natural light and to model the space, which is crowned with an arched skylight that runs the length of the room. A gallery on the second floor affords views down into this space.

In a variation on a theme, De Vido's design for the Frocht House, also in East Hampton, uses a gable form to define the central space, which runs as a cross axis to the house's linear arrangement. A bridge traverses this great space, affording views into the living room and the entry hall. For the client, this space at the heart serves as a gallery for a diverse art collection.

Pure Geometries

Squares, triangles, rectangles, and circles—perceived both in plan and in section—weave their way through De Vido's architecture. The architect's fascination with pure geometries and proportional composition—the classical foundations of architecture that he learned under Jean Labatut at Princeton—result in anything but simple buildings. Geometry is the seed of rational organization, a rigor in many of these projects that frames the observer's perception of the architecture and the inhabitants' view of the world.

In the Sametz House in Garrison, New York, for example, the perfectly square plan is projected in three dimensions into a space-containing cube. Although this house has shed roofs, decks, and large glazed areas, the geometry of the cube is preserved, particularly on the exterior, where the cornice traces the cube's outline where the volume is violated to create exterior spaces. Punctures within the cube frame views of the nearby Hudson River.

A variation on the cube is found in the West House in East Hampton, New York, in which diagonal slices are carved through the form. Inside, the sculpted form can be read through the exposed roof structure. The Sheehy House, also in East Hampton, is composed of cubic volumes joined by a bridge that links the primary living areas with the guest wing. On the exterior, De Vido plays a variation on the building's geometric theme with a composition of rectangular wall surfaces, windows, and voids. The horizontal siding reiterates the building's linear design.

Compared to Sheehy, the Quinones/Bieganek House—yet another East Hampton project—takes the idea of joined cubes further. Here the tether is a diagonal element containing circulation and service spaces that slices through the building's geometry and is expressed on the exterior with strong gable forms. Color is used vigorously to underscore the building's complex geometry.

Respect for Context

Context as an inspiration for design is treated with respect, not veneration—a distinction that allows for creativity without slavishly following the patterns of the past. As one might expect, De Vido's strongest contextual responses are found in buildings situated in dense urban fabrics. One such project is for a townhouse at 222 Columbia Heights in Brooklyn, New York, in the midst of a Landmarks Preservation District. The neighborhood is noted for its four-story brownstones, many dating from the late 1800s. De Vido created a new building of similar height and mass, its window treatment and placement echoing the fenestration of the older structures. Belt courses and cornices articulate the facade in a fashion similar to the context. A design award from the New York State Association of Architects cited the project for its "skillful and sensitive response to the challenging problem of relating new construction to an historic district."

A very different context and response is found in the Matthews House in East Hampton, New York, which is sited at the bluff of a hill overlooking Gardiner's Bay. In its scale, form, and materials, this house recalls the seaside architecture of the region, yet the building is thoroughly Modern, particularly in its open, two-story interior. The design, which won a National Honor Award from the American Institute of Architects, was lauded for being "a good example of contemporary Cape Cod." Yet another approach is found in De Vido's design for the Queens Theatre in the Park, an adaptation of a structure originally designed by Philip Johnson for the 1964 World's Fair. The building was a simple concrete drum. De Vido added a lobby, stairs, and an elevator, all contained in a concrete and glass-block addition that was faithful to the existing architecture. Breathing life into the old building, the new elements also echo the forms and colors found in other fair buildings nearby.

Conclusion

Study the architecture in this beautiful monograph and you are sure to find other themes that unify De Vido's work in addition to the five described above. Across the span of his career, De Vido's buildings contain many of the qualities that make architecture timeless: proportion, rhythm, spatial sequence, sensitivity to human scale, and an intelligent use of materials. The site, the particulars of the program, the clients' wishes and dreams (and their pocketbooks) are also important generators of form. The full measure of Alfredo De Vido's variegated search for design excellence and the unified variety of his work come through on every page.

Michael J. Crosbie is a senior architect with Steven Winter Associates and an adjunct professor of architecture at Roger Williams University. The author of several books on architecture and hundreds of articles in various professional journals, Dr Crosbie lives with his family in the small New England village of Essex, Connecticut, USA.

Work Places

Work places can usefully be divided into
various types: shops and stores, restaurants
and cafes, offices and industrial buildings.
With stores or restaurants, it is important
to present an image that will convey a
sense of confidence to the consumer in
the product being sold. Good lighting and
clean, easy-to-maintain materials that look
inviting are essential. Easy access to service
counters and display units must also be
considered. Close liaison should be
maintained with the owners to ensure
the facility is responsive to consumers.

Lee's Art Shop

Design/Completion 1976/1976
New York, New York
Lee's Art Shop
7,500 square feet
Ceramic tiles, painted plaster vaults, steel scaffolding for display racks, demountable counter system

The owner had built a successful retail business serving the many architectural offices and advertising agencies in the area, as well as students at the nearby Art Students League. He now wished to expand his retail space tenfold.

Not wanting to move out of the area, he found a Gothic Revival-style building across the street, with handsome vaulted ceilings and ornamental plasterwork. To preserve this setting, the architects devised an open plan scheme that allows shoppers to browse. The merchandise is grouped into three departments—framing, fine arts, and commercial—with easily damaged goods such as paper and boards being placed behind the counters.

Pipe scaffolding is used to hang lights, signs, and colorful graphics. To attract customers, the architects articulated the street front with a series of angled glass panes.

The new store combines elegance and modern display techniques to create an attractive setting for customers.

1 Plan
2 Street front
3 Entrance sales area
4&5 Main circulation route
6&7 Detail of display systems

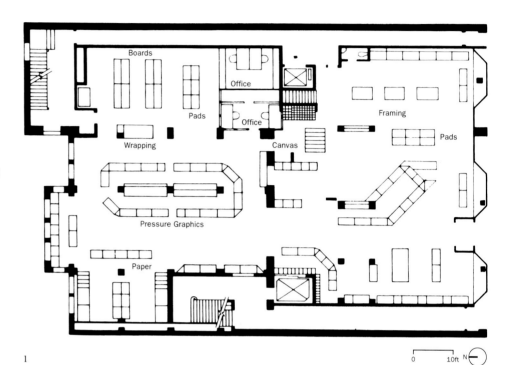

1

2

3

4

5

6

7

Church's English Shoes

Design/Completion 1995/1995
New York, New York
Church's English Shoes
1,050 square feet
Cherry and mahogany casework, carpet, lighting

This Madison Avenue store has been New York's leading outlet for Church's English Shoes for many years. The aim of the design was to add space for an expanded line of merchandise and a boutique for specialty shoes.

Wood was selected for the main cabinetry and the architects made an effort to blend the new addition's details with those of the existing store.

1 Street front
2 Main sales area
3 Women's boutique
4 Renovated historic store

3

1

2

4

Berk of Burlington Arcade

Design/Completion 1987/1987
New York, New York
David Berk Ltd
885 square feet
Custom wood display cabinets and air distribution devices, carpet

When Berk of Burlington Arcade, a long-established British firm selling cashmeres, planned to open a branch store on Madison Avenue, the owners requested the ambience of a traditional shop. Rather than responding with a strict reproduction of an English shop, the architects sought to convey its characteristic atmosphere.

The store fixtures are of lustrous cherry wood, divided into pigeon-hole units suitable for storing sweaters and other items. Above these cabinets, a louvered cornice of the same cherry wood conceals air conditioning ducts. Traditional brass rails display hanging garments, and a bright red carpet completes the palette. The lighting is balanced to show true colors.

The store is in a designated landmark area, so it was required that the storefront restoration be historically accurate. It was given approval by the New York City Landmarks Preservation Commission.

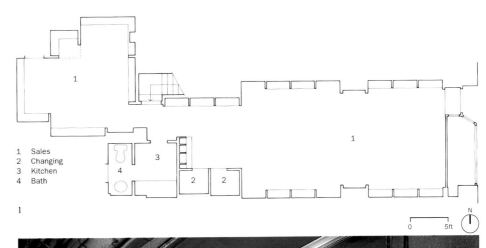

1 Sales
2 Changing
3 Kitchen
4 Bath

1

0   5ft

2

1 Plan
2 Show window
3 Interior
4 Detail view

3   4

Tess

Design/Completion 1987/1987
New York, New York
Tess Corp.
1,065 square feet
Stained wood slats covering mechanical equipment on ceiling, ceramic floor tiles, mirrors, neon, stock pull-down security gates for clothing display

A well-lit, adaptable sales space was required for a small showroom on New York's Seventh Avenue. At the entrance, a neon sign spells out the firm's name in bright green letters through the glass door. Inside, the space flows from entry to sales area and then to offices, which look back on the entire room.

To unify the multi-purpose room, the architects proposed a vaulted wooden ceiling running its entire length. The ceiling conceals unsightly air conditioning equipment and the concrete structure above it.

Walls in the sales area are covered with stock aluminum storefront grating, permitting clothing to be displayed on hangers and changed as desired. Low-voltage halogen lighting provides true color and may be switched on in various combinations to highlight specific areas.

Off-white walls combine with whitened natural wood cabinetry, ceiling, and furniture to form a background against which colorful fashions are displayed. A blue-green chair rail serves as a horizontal accent.

1 Entry
2 Showroom
3 Director
4 Sales
5 Administrative

0   5ft

N

1 Plan
2 Entrance area
3 Main sales and display area
4 Detail view

2

3

4

Catherine Atzen Day Spa

Design/Completion 1985/1985
New York, New York
Catherine Atzen
1,870 square feet
Tile, sheetrock, plastic laminate cabinets, glass display case

The client planned a beauty salon and spa on the East Side of Manhattan. While the location was excellent, the property itself had a dark, somber facade and a small display window. In addition, the store had a two-story facade which was built out to the sidewalk property line, creating an awkward connection with the building behind it.

To solve this problem, the architects designed a two-story storefront that combines white metal and tall, thin pieces of glass with vertical mullions, narrowly spaced. Behind this facade the original openings in the brownstone were restored. This design solution succeeded in unifying the appearance of the building and store and also let light penetrate into the shop's upper rooms.

The salon interior features liberal use of white tiles, with soft blue accents. On both floors an arched ceiling provides a sense of extra height. The overall effect is one of cleanliness and good health.

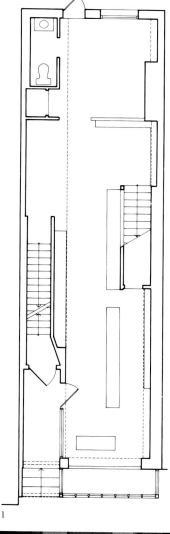

1

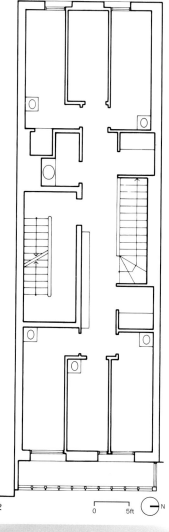

2

0   5ft   N

3

4

5

6

7

1 First floor plan
2 Second floor plan
3&4 Exterior views
5 Main floor entrance
6&7 Detail views

Word of Mouth/Cafe Word of Mouth

Design/Completion 1979/1979 (take out store); 1992/1992 (cafe)
New York, New York
Christi Finch
1,500 square feet (store); 1,350 square feet (cafe)
Store: tile floors and vaulted ceiling, industrial fixtures, bent electrical conduit fixtures, custom display cabinets
Cafe: custom chairs and tables, sheetrock walls trimmed with wood, custom ceramic tile floor, painted wood storefront, custom lighting fixtures

The owner of a popular catering and delicacies shop housed in an old New York brownstone on the Upper East Side of Manhattan needed additional kitchen and retail space and decided to relocate nearby. To retain the character and intimate quality of the original store, the architects used design details that recalled food shops and kitchens of 19th century England. The storefront is made up of small panes of glass through which passers-by can see food displays and watch food preparation.

A vaulted ceiling of terra cotta tiles gives a special character to the store. Tile, stainless steel, butcher block, and formica finishes were chosen for easy maintenance. The resulting workspace is efficient and attractive.

Some 13 years later, when the owner decided to open a cafe upstairs, the architects were again commissioned. The resulting design integrates the facade and interior details with the earlier shop below. The grid on the facade is continued and enlivened with curves, stained glass, and pennants.

In the cafe, walls were decorated with pilasters and chair rails, and crowned by a domed ceiling over the dining area. A patterned tile floor enhances the area. Lighting and furniture were designed by the architects.

1

2

3

1 Front detail
2 Entrance
3 Exterior before cafe addition
4 Street view

4

5 Ground floor sales area
6 View from open kitchen
7 Behind counter
8 Working drawing
9 First floor plan
10 Second floor plan (cafe)
11 Cafe from entry

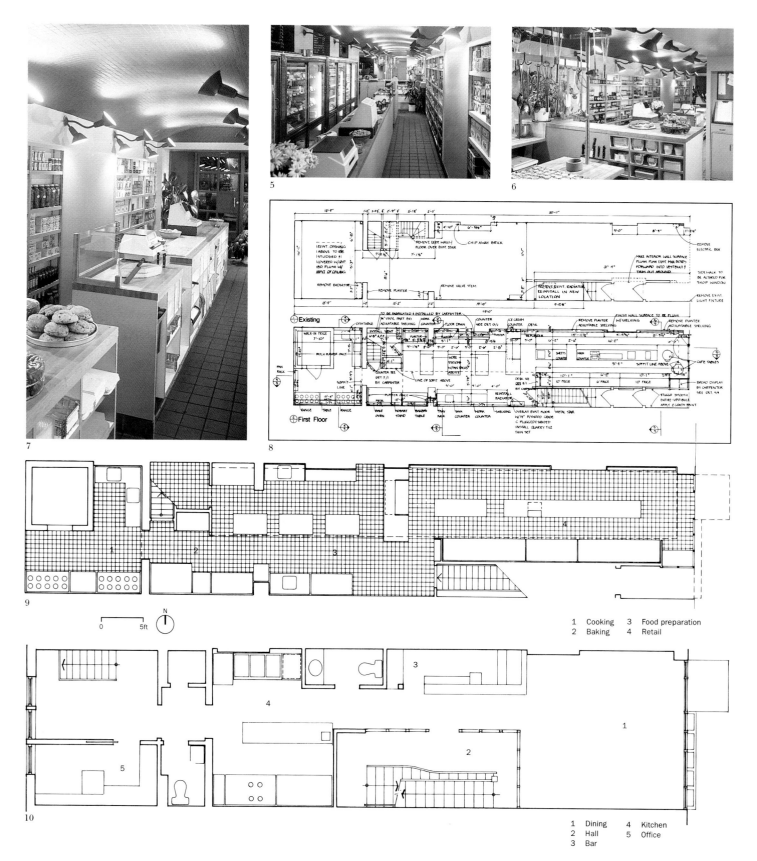

7

8

9

1 Cooking   3 Food preparation
2 Baking   4 Retail

0   5ft   N

10

1 Dining   4 Kitchen
2 Hall   5 Office
3 Bar

11

12

12   Architect-designed furniture
13   Detail including architect-designed lighting

13

Stuarts Restaurant

Design/Completion 1985/1985
Manhattan, New York
Stuarts Restaurant Co.
3,700 square feet
Hung painted plywood boxes housing mechanical systems and custom
lighting; carpet; wood furniture; upholstered custom banquettes; recycled
wood bar; mirrors

The space available for Stuarts, a 250-seat Manhattan restaurant, had been carved out of the first floors of a new high-rise apartment and two adjacent older residential buildings. The architects had to fit the restaurant into this space without restricting access to the apartments above. Since the apartment doors and stairs were in the middle of the buildings, the solution was to build around the entry.

The resulting plan is an inverted "U" with a large dining room to one side at the rear and a bar/restaurant area facing the street. Doors can be opened up in fine weather. The restaurant continues behind hallways and connects with the kitchen/ service area which runs parallel to the bar. Tucked in the rear, facing a court, is a large dining room which can be closed off for large private parties or shut completely on quiet evenings.

The outside is painted a glossy dark green; the awning is also dark green with cream-colored lettering. The interior features hung ceiling panels that serve to conceal lighting fixtures and mechanical equipment. The bar and entrance are enhanced by richly toned wood, while the dining areas are painted a light cream color. Wood trim, mirrors, and lighting sconces enliven the elegant room.

1

1   Street view
2   Entry
3   Plan
4   Main dining
5   Bar

2

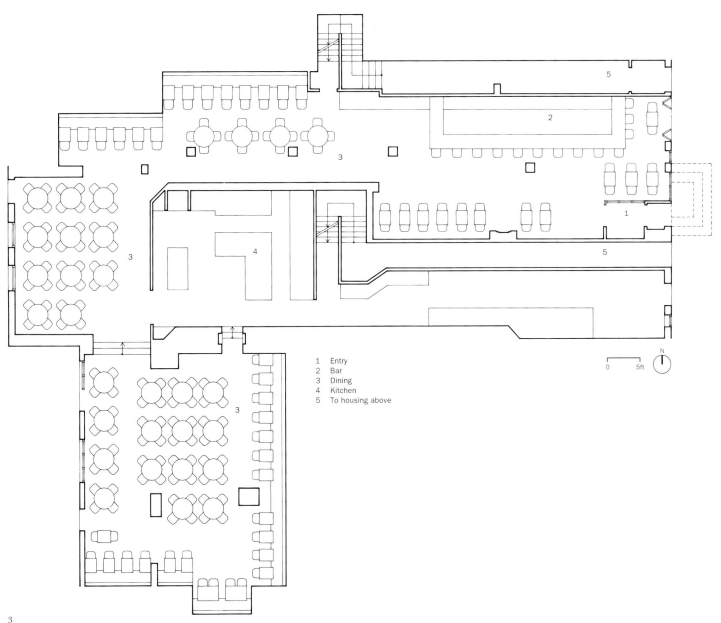

3

1 Entry
2 Bar
3 Dining
4 Kitchen
5 To housing above

0   5ft

N

4

5

La Chausseria

Design/Completion 1985/1985
Manhattan, New York
La Chausseria Corp.
750 square feet
Carpet, shoe display system, acoustical tiles, aluminum storefront, canvas awning

For reasons of efficiency and good merchandising, the display system used in La Chausseria presents the French company's entire range of women's shoes on wall-hung racks. All colors, lengths, and widths are on display (left shoe only), allowing the customer to browse the range and try on selected shoes. Customers only need to seek help from a salesperson once they have made an initial selection. This system frees salespeople to serve additional customers, permitting the store to run efficiently with fewer sales staff.

The architects lit the merchandise from above and below with fluorescent lights set within a colonnade on each side of the room. Lightly textured gray walls provide a contrasting background to the merchandise. Low benches in the middle of the room are for the comfort of customers.

On the exterior, columns echo the interior motif and an awning carries the company's logotype.

1   Plan
2   Shoe display
3&4   Interior views
5   Exterior

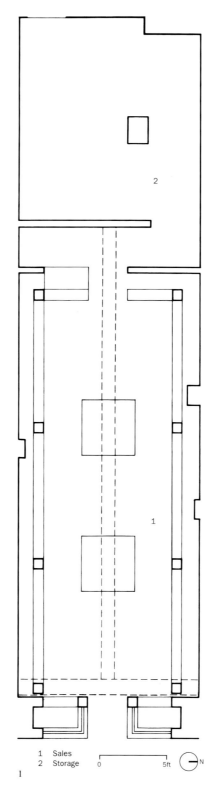

1

1   Sales
2   Storage

0   5ft   N

2

3

4

J.J. Lally Chinese Art

Design/Completion 1992/1992
New York, New York
J.J. Lally & Co.
1,950 square feet
Carpeted floors, custom maple display cabinets with adjustable lighting,
track and recessed lighting, painted sheetrock walls and hung ceiling

To show off the collection of Chinese antiquities to their best advantage, flexible and dramatic lighting was required. A system was designed within each case that provides light from the front, back, bottom, and sides. Natural wood was used to complement the generally rich earthen hues of ancient pottery and weathered bronze. Dark green walls give added depth to the display cases.

The design of the L-shaped gallery allows it to be divided into two areas, while a centrally located reception area overlooks the entire gallery and permits visitors to be guided as required. Behind the scenes, offices, a work area, and a library/conference room are conveniently located. From the public hall outside the gallery, a glimpse of the antiquities is revealed through glass doors.

1

2

3

4

1&2   Interior views
  3   Display cabinet
  4   Interior
  5   Plan
  6   Entry

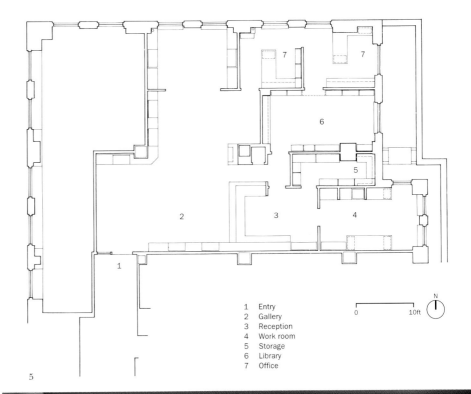

5

1   Entry
2   Gallery
3   Reception
4   Work room
5   Storage
6   Library
7   Office

0   10ft

N

6

Wig Shop

Design/Completion 1980/1981
New York, New York
Jacques Darcel Inc.
1,620 square feet
Wood flooring, painted sheetrock, laminate cabinets, mirrors,
built-in seating

Despite its long, narrow shape, the wig shop has been zoned to provide generous display space for merchandise, space for fitting and work, and privacy for customers.

The zones are divided by a shaped soffit across the ceiling, which not only screens the lighting but also avoids the tunnel-like effect which would otherwise be created by the shop's elongated shape.

To provide an exterior area for display, the entrance is recessed and a reception/waiting area is provided nearby. Mirrors are provided for customer use and to give a greater sense of space.

Wall finishes of white formica and a wood parquet floor serve as a backdrop for the displays.

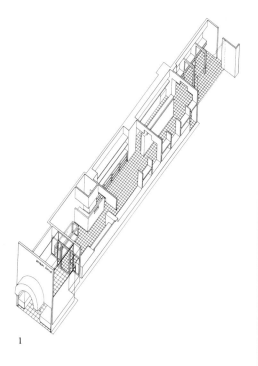

1

1 Axonometric
2 Exterior
3 Interior

2

3

Troa Cho Boutique

Design/Completion 1982/1982
New York, New York
Troa Cho Inc.
1,700 square feet
Stained and finished wood floor, painted wood display units,
concealed indirect lighting

The building chosen by the owner of this boutique as the site for her newest store was located in the Upper East Side Historic District, a Landmarks Preservation Area.

Since there was little precedent for a store on the ground floor of a 19th century brownstone, the architects designed an operable display case that visually joins the two openings to the store. It is columnar in shape, recalling an earlier era, and supports an illuminated sign carrying the owner's name. The design was deemed appropriate by the New York City Landmarks Commission.

The interior employs this same columnar element in the form of free-standing display cases and inset wall panels for clothes hanging. Pale gray and yellow finishes provide a subdued backdrop for the designer's clothing.

1   Plan and section
2   Exterior
3   Exterior in context
4–6   Interior views

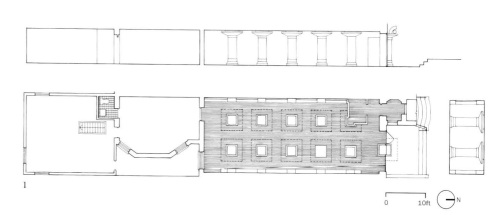

1

2

3

4

5

6

Ranch 1 Fast Food Restaurant

Design/Completion 1997/1997
Stamford, Connecticut
Ranch 1
1,950 square feet
Ceramic tile floors, sheetrock and ceramic tile walls, sheetrock ceilings, ceramic counter faces, butcher block countertops, backlit painted wood frieze

The architects were commissioned to design a facility for Ranch 1, a new chain of fast food restaurants, in the Stamford Mall in Stamford, Connecticut. The mall has many restrictive covenants and the Ranch 1 company also had criteria which had to be observed. Within those guidelines, the architects designed a simple food serving and seating area.

To illustrate the kind of food offered by Ranch 1, the architects designed a cartoon-like chicken cut-out which is featured in a backlit frieze outside the restaurant, facing the mall promenade, and inside the restaurant, encircling the serving counter.

The yellow, black, and white color scheme and the colorful photos of the meals are part of Ranch 1's nationwide identity.

1

2

3

1 Mall view
2 Detail of counter
3 Mall view
4 Entrance

4

Offices for Import Associates Inc.

Design/Completion 1976/1977
New York, New York
Norman Mercer
5,000 square feet
Custom display cases of glass and laminate,
custom carpet, sheetrock, custom reception desk

The client, an importer of shoes and
clothing, moved to the World Trade
Center and requested office space for staff
as well as room to display the firm's line
of goods. The chairman also wanted
to display his firm's collection of ship
models, symbolizing the international
nature of the business.

A bright, airy gallery links the elevators
and the senior executive area and provides
display space for the collection of ship
models. This route also offers glimpses
of computers, telex machines, and work
spaces. Open office planning is part
of the design.

2

1

3

4

5

1 Reception desk
2 Diagonal circulation
3 Conference room
4&5 Interior views

Muir, Cornelius, Moore Office Renovation

Design/Completion 1985/1985
New York, New York
Muir, Cornelius, Moore
500 square feet
Sheetrock walls with color inserts, custom lighting and carpet,
custom desk, leather upholstery on furniture

The 500-square-foot reception lobby for Muir, Cornelius, Moore, a graphic design firm in Manhattan, was once little more than a T-shaped standard elevator lobby in a midtown skyscraper. The aim was to achieve a design that was simple, elegant, and functional.

The renovation established a new identity for the office, primarily by means of a recurring grid. The walls have two-and-a-half inch square coffers cut into them at intervals of 18 inches. The vertical inside surfaces of each coffer are painted strong shades of blue and red, giving the wall a tapestry-like dimension and character. The dimensions of the dot-pattern grid in the modular carpet tiles match those of the wall. The grid also appears in the tufting of the leather-covered club chairs designed by Josef Hoffmann.

1 Reception
2 Detail
3 Conference room
4 Reception

70 East 10th Street, New York

Design/Completion 1990/1991
New York, New York
70 East 10th Street Co-op
4,300 square feet (lobby); 14,500 square feet (garden/entrance)
Interiors: stipple paint finishes on sheetrock; furnishings and carpet by architect; custom lighting
Garden/exterior: concrete canopy with glass block roof inserts; precast concrete and stone pavers; garden furniture; planting for low maintenance in a city environment

Designed in the 1950s, this 425-unit cooperative apartment house was due for restoration. The co-op board requested that the architects redesign the canopy, the entire entrance and garden court, the lobby and ground floor corridors, and the south- and east-facing gardens.

In the lobby and corridors, new lighting was installed in place of outdated fixtures that gave little light and were energy-inefficient. New furniture and fabrics were selected and new carpets were designed, incorporating subtle colors and textures in a geometric pattern. Existing marble was refinished and a new color scheme was implemented. Existing terrazzo floors were repaired and polished.

In the gardens, a new paving system was installed, perennial plantings were provided, and comfortable benches and chairs furnished. In the front entrance court, existing trees were pruned to enhance their shapes and colorful flowering annuals were planted beneath them.

The existing concrete canopy at the front entrance was replaced with one that allows natural light to penetrate through a pattern of glass blocks. The deteriorated sidewalks and driveway were repaved with concrete pavers in a decorative design.

Exterior lighting was brought up to date in both the front and rear gardens for the residents' enjoyment in the evening hours. Security was also enhanced with a new system of attractive fences and barriers.

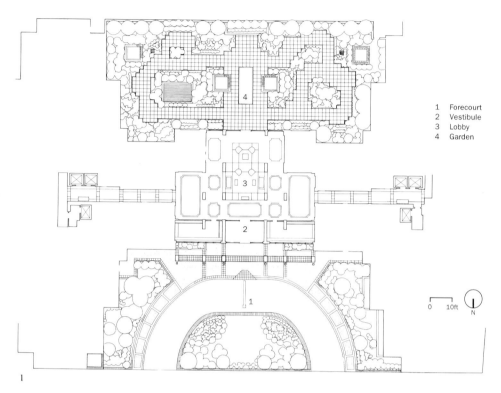

1 Forecourt
2 Vestibule
3 Lobby
4 Garden

0 10ft N

1 Plan
2 Entrance drive
3 Rear garden
4 Corridor
5 Lobby
6 Porte cochere

4

5

6

Lobby Renovation, 108 East 16th Street

Design/Completion 1990/1990
New York, New York
250 square feet
Painted wood storefront, marble interior with inserts of tile on frieze, painted trim, existing original cast-iron column painted black and dramatically lit

The ground floor of this 1920s building had been awkwardly modernized in the 1950s by placing metal paneling over the carved stonework. The architects stripped off the metal cladding, cleaned and restored the stonework, and provided an open lobby and storefront in harmony with the building.

Color was introduced into the storefront, and wood and various shades of marble were utilized in the new lobby. New lighting, a directory, and cushioned seating at the entrance completed the renovation.

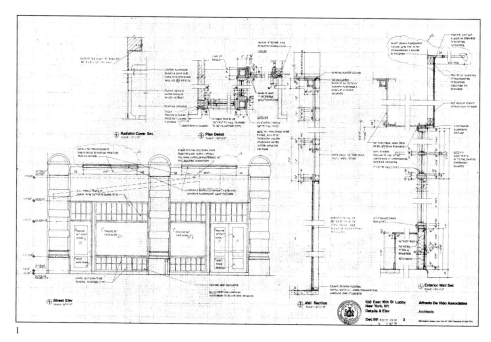

1

2

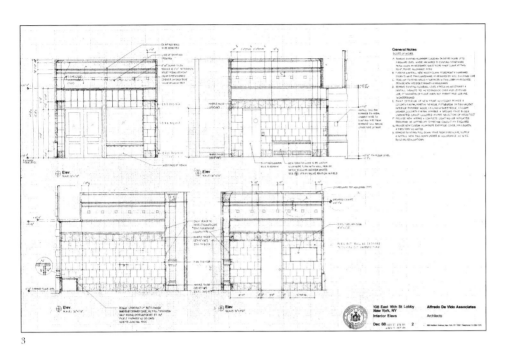

3

4

5

1   Working drawings
2   Exterior
3   Working drawings
4&5 Interior views

Architect's Office, 699 Madison Avenue

Design/Completion 1978/1978
New York, New York
Alfredo De Vido
800 square feet
Tubular frames of electrical conduit and store fixture
fittings, steel shelving, wood and laminate shelving,
carpet, industrial lighting fixtures

A basic pipe system was employed so that
furniture, storage, and space dividers
could be designed using the same light,
economical components. Along with the
steel shelves, formica tops, and plywood
dividers, the pipe system provides the
needed storage and work surface areas.
Stock storage is set within the basic pipe
framework.

Office walls are painted in shades of gray,
set off by a ceiling of white and yellow.

1

2

1–4   Interior views

3

4

WebGenesis

Design/Completion 1997/1997
New York, New York
WebGenesis
6,000 square feet
Sheetrock and glass block partitions, exposed ductwork and lighting, carpet

This project provides offices for a web site design and operation center in midtown Manhattan. The facility contains a room for 50 network servers and a series of cubicles for the use of WebGenesis staff and customers.

Since the interchange of information among staff is a key part of the company's work process, the atmosphere is planned to be open, informal, and collegial. A round room functions as the circulation center between two elevator banks, evoking the company's "world-embracing" circular logo.

From the round room, two radial interior "streets" provide access to the cubicles. Within the cubicles, indirect uplighting provides optimal conditions for viewing computer monitors. At each end of the "streets" are lounges and conference areas.

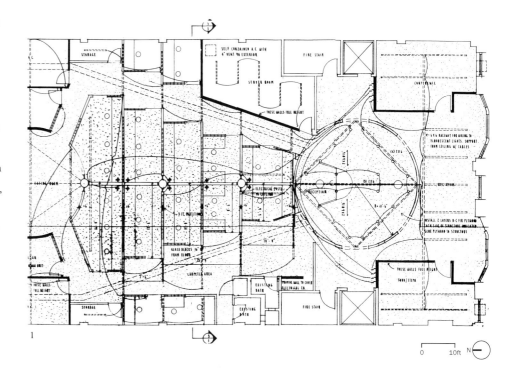

1

0   10ft   N

1   Plan
2&3   Entrance area
4   Work area from entrance
5&6   Work carrels
7   Diagonal corridors from entrance area

2

3

4

5

6

7

Allendale Park Modular Industrial Buildings

Design/Completion 1977/1979
Allendale, New Jersey
Allendale Park Corp.
Site area: 15 acres
Textured concrete block, standard bar joist construction,
aluminum windows

Careful site planning to preserve existing trees and tight control over design elements resulted in an attractive industrial park. The architects worked closely with the design/build team of Lev Zetlin Associates and Diesel Construction to produce industrial buildings that would attract desirable tenants and fit comfortably within a predominantly residential community.

These goals were achieved by limiting the palette of materials and carefully locating the design elements, such as windows, entrances, loading docks, and mechanical equipment. The result is a group of industrial buildings which are fully occupied and yield higher rentals than those in surrounding areas.

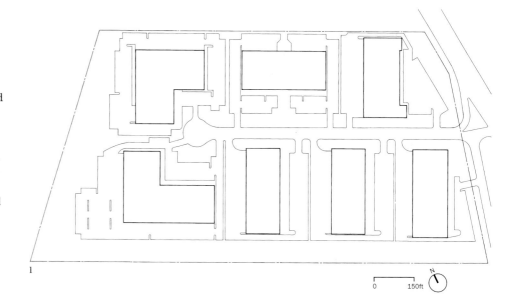

1

0 150ft N

2

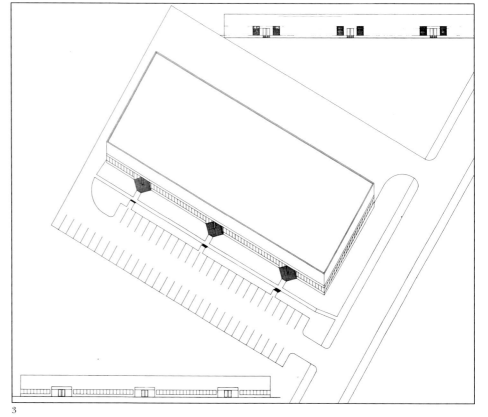

3

1 Site plan
2 Typical entrance
3 Axonometric
4 Elevation studies
5 View from park entrance

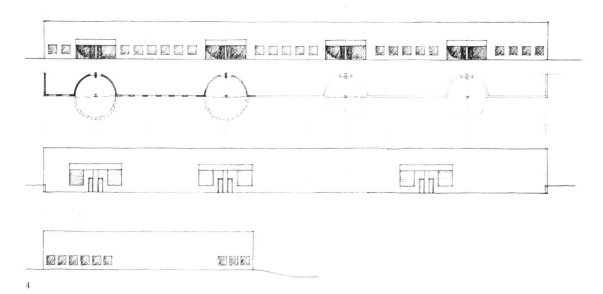

4

5

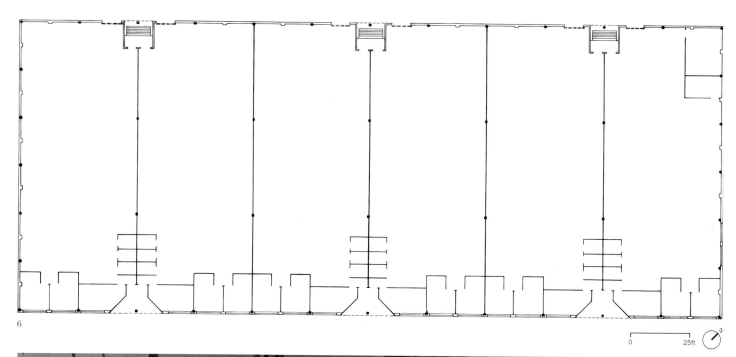

6

0   25ft

7

6   Typical building plan
7   Exterior

Evidence Vehicle Facility

Design/Completion 1996/1996
Red Hook, Brooklyn, New York
New York City Police Department
7,200 square feet (administration building); 54,000 square feet
(warehouse) (site area: 15 acres)
Textured concrete block, glazed concrete block, concrete floors,
Dryvit exterior for signage and accent areas, hung sheetrock and
acoustical ceilings

The site, on a disused waterfront in Brooklyn, was selected for an Evidence Vehicle Facility for the New York City Police Department. The site plan includes parking areas for vehicles used in criminal activities and subsequently impounded by the police, construction of a new administration building, and rehabilitation of a warehouse for vehicles used in serious crimes.

The administration building includes space for electronic equipment, offices, locker rooms, and a security counter for paperwork and the payment of fines. In the warehouse renovation, a continuous roof monitor was provided to introduce natural light.

The materials are simple, durable, and economical. Split-face concrete block, glazed block in New York City colors, and a sign of Dryvit add liveliness to this utilitarian building.

1

2

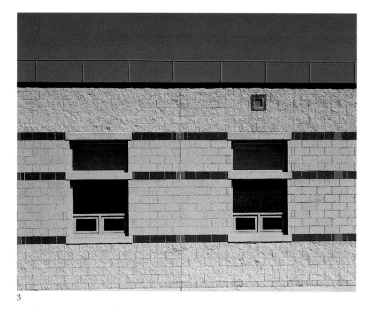

3

4

Previous page:
1 Entrance
2 Exterior

3 Detail
4 Renovated warehouse
5 Exterior

5

NEW YORK POLICE DEPARTMENT
ERIE BASIN
EVIDENCE VEHICLE FACILITY

Silver Sands State Park

Design/Completion 1990/2000
Milford, Connecticut
State of Connecticut
20,000 square feet (buildings); 310 acres (total park development)
Post and beam wood construction with heavy plank skin and wood shingle
exterior sheathing; fiberglass skylights; treated wood walkways and piling

This project redevelops an existing state
park which was underutilized for many
years due to a lack of maintenance.
The project seeks to create sustainable
recreational areas along the beaches,
preserve wetlands and marsh areas, and
adapt the park to the existing landfill.

The built structures include a bathhouse,
containing a restaurant and changing,
toilet, first aid, and storage facilities;
an administrative building which houses
repair, maintenance, and administrative
functions; as well as pavilions, boardwalks,
and covered lookouts.

1

2

SILVER SANDS STATE PARK

Alfredo De Vido Associates

Architects

1   Aerial view showing complete development plans
2   Rendering of bathhouse central facility

Gathering Places

People gather with a commonality of
purpose to see, participate, believe, and
learn. The architect is called upon to
provide a focal point for the assembly as
well as good vision, acoustics, and lighting.

Wolf Trap Farm Park

Design/Completion 1969/1971
Vienna, Virginia
National Park Service
Wood trusses covering available seating area, open sides
with wood acoustical reflecting panels, steel-framed stage
house sheathed with heavy timber planking, concrete stepped
floor for undercover seating area

A 130-acre site of undisturbed rolling country in Fairfax County, Virginia, near Washington, DC, was chosen as the venue for relaxed summer concerts for audiences of up to 6,500.

Various hurdles faced the architects in realizing this vision: acoustic reception had to be good in all seats and on the surrounding lawns, as did visual contact with the performers; noises from an expressway and adjacent parking had to be kept to a minimum; and all this had to be done on a budget of $3 million and with minimal disruption of the site.

The resulting design is a wood roof resting on 154-foot-long composite queen post trusses and arranged so as to project a balanced sound from the stage to the huge audience. About half the audience is seated under this shell—1,000 of them in a balcony and the rest in a seating arrangement that follows the slope of the ground. The remaining concert-goers sit on the lawns outside but can see and hear as well as those inside. A series of free-standing side baffles helps reinforce the sound.

The stage house is on two levels: the stage proper above; changing rooms, rehearsal rooms, and offices below. Natural red cedar cladding ties the whole structure together and harmonizes with the natural site.

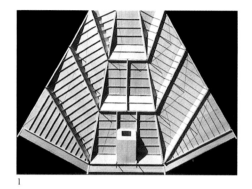
1

2

3

4

5

1&2   Models of structural roof design
3–5   Exterior views
6   View through reflective side panels

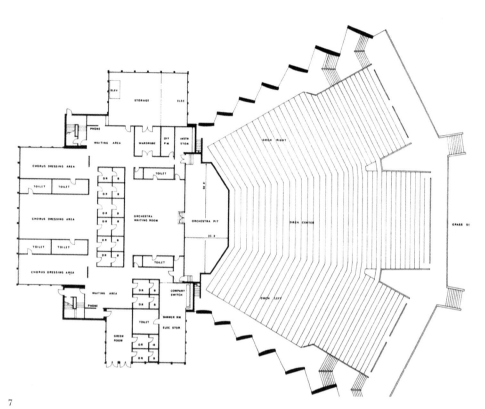

7

9

10

11

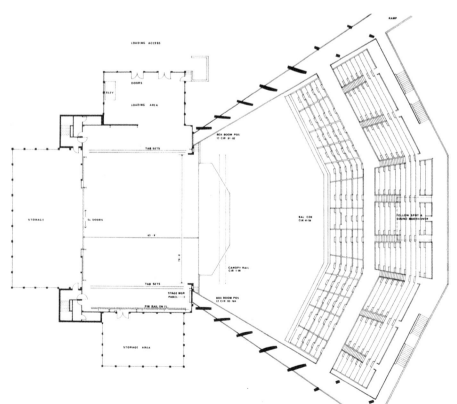

8

7 Ground floor plan
8 Balcony plan
9 Roof panel detail
10–12 Interior views

Mann Music Center

Design/Completion 1974/1976
Philadelphia, Pennsylvania
The City of Philadelphia
Steel frame covered with wood planking and metal roof

The site chosen for this summer home of the Philadelphia Symphony Orchestra was the city's central open space—Fairmount Park. The shell had to provide covered seating for 5,000, and twice as many again had to be able to see and hear from the adjacent lawns.

With the need for good acoustics and a relaxed setting in mind, the architects and their acoustical consultant designed a mammoth shell of open-web steel joists with a wood plank ceiling. The geometry of the building and the orchestra shell is designed for natural sound transmission within the structure; an amplifying system is provided for those sitting outside.

The sides of the building are open, offering concert-goers framed views of the park and city. Access and departure are taken care of comfortably by a series of wide, light, flying ramps and outdoor stairs. Ambient noise from city streets and latecomers' parking is reduced by an earth berm which acts as a sound screen.

Under the 14,000-square-foot stage are a green room, dressing rooms, and offices. The entire shell is finished on the outside with a crisp coat of terne-clad steel.

1

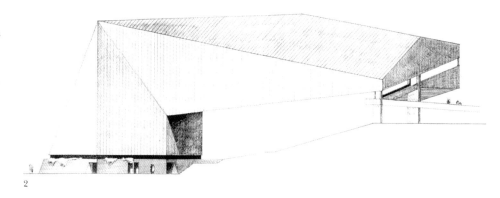

2

3

1   Site plan
2   Sketch of elevation
3   Model photo
4&5 Side views
6   Rear view

4

5

6

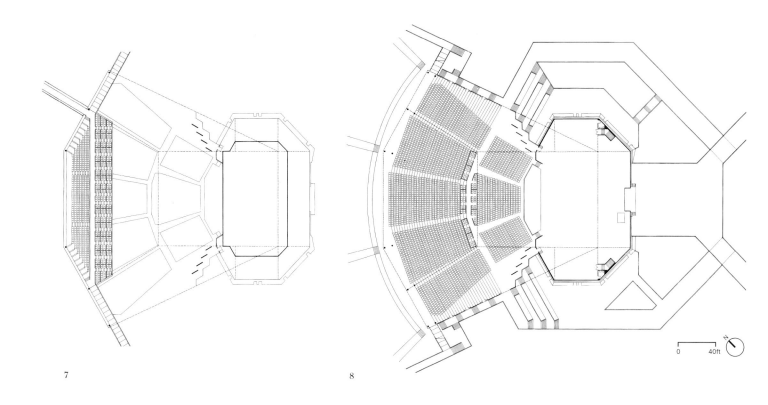

7

8

0   40ft

9

10

7   Balcony plan
8   Main floor plan
9   Exterior from uphill
10 Interior
11 Section
12–15 Exterior views
16 Interior
17 Interior towards balcony

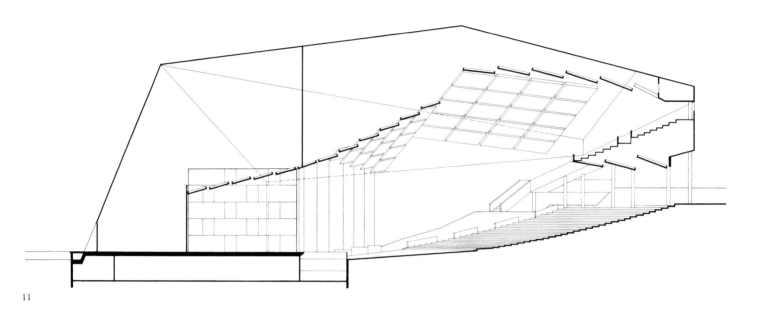

11

12

13

14

15

16

17

Brooklyn Academy of Music Renovation

Design/Completion 1968/1969
Brooklyn, New York
Brooklyn Academy of Music (BAM)
Renovation of lobby and existing hall

The lobby of this grand old concert hall had deteriorated, especially its unique marble mosaic floor. In the auditorium itself, the seats showed the effects of 25 years of wear, and the lighting and stage equipment had become outdated and inefficient.

The architects were able to restore these public spaces, as well as some administrative offices, to their former richness. The lobby's vaults were repaired and repainted, new chandeliers designed, kiosks installed, and the box offices and marble mosaic floors restored. Within the hall, new seats and carpets were installed, walls restored, and stage equipment improved and supplemented. Lighting was replaced and new fixtures were added.

The building was successfully modernized without detracting from its turn of the century character.

1

1   Audience area showing renovated lights
2   Lobby showing restored historic floor
3   Architect-designed chandeliers and ceiling restoration
4   Restored auditorium

2

3

4

Manhattan School of Music Renovation/Addition

Design/Completion 1968/1969
New York, New York
Manhattan School of Music
30,000 square feet
Concrete, stone veneer, glass, aluminum window frames,
carpet, ceramic and vinyl tiles

When the architects were asked to rehabilitate the former Juilliard School of Music into a new home for the Manhattan School of Music, they saw at once that a key design goal was to evoke a "sense of place" for the new school, not merely convert the previous school's building. The focus for the school was to be a new student and activities center within the old building, and a new addition housing a cafeteria. To achieve this, some interior walls were removed, and the bookstore and staff offices were grouped around the new cafeteria and lounge. The cafeteria itself opens on a private landscaped courtyard—an oasis within an otherwise congested urban area.

Following the client's brief, the existing auditorium and library were completely rehabilitated, and the entire building was air-conditioned to isolate practice areas from distracting street noises.

1

2

1 Exterior of building showing new addition
2 Addition and walled garden
3 Cafeteria
4 Stair
5 Exterior
6&7 Cafeteria interior

3

4

5

6

7

8

10

9

8   Corridor in student center
9   Renovated auditorium with architect-designed
      chandelier
10   Student center

Henry and Edsel Ford Auditorium Renovation

Design 1976
Detroit, Michigan
Detriot Symphony Orchestra
Site area: 5 acres
Existing structure of concrete and concrete block, steel roof trusses,
all covered with sheetrock and plaster

Over the years, acoustic deficiencies in Detroit's Henry and Edsel Ford Auditorium came to include lack of volume, poor bass response, and poor overall sound quality. The board of directors of the Detroit Symphony Orchestra invited the architects and their acoustical consultant to propose an interior renovation that would improve the hall's acoustics, and to show how this could be accomplished over a three-year period.

The recommendations were that the existing interior finishes be removed to expand the building's volume to the outer walls and roof, and that a lattice of metal tubes be inserted within this volume to screen the existing columns, beams, and mechanical equipment while permitting sound to pass through.

The design also involved moving the orchestra forward into the audience for greater immediacy, and constructing a new shell and other reflective surfaces which would be sufficiently dense to develop a good sound quality.

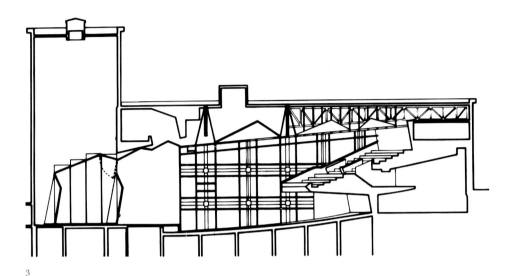

3

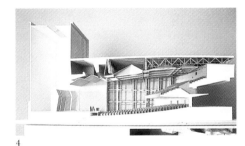

1

0   40ft

2

5

7

6

1&2   Plans
  3   Section
4–7   Photographs of model proposals

Queens Theatre in the Park

Design/Completion 1992/1993
New York, New York
New York City Department of Cultural Affairs/
Borough of Queens
24,352 square feet on two floors
including two mezzanines
Reinforced concrete, precast concrete rings,
various reflective surfaces or absorptive material,
exterior opening solid glass blocks

The Queens Theatre in the Park brought new life to the New York State Pavilion, designed by Philip Johnson for the 1964 World's Fair, at Flushing Meadows/ Corona Park in New York City. Originally known as "Theaterama," the building was a 40-foot-high 100-foot-diameter concrete drum designed for slide viewing. It was designated for conversion to a theater by the New York City Department of Cultural Affairs and the Borough of Queens.

The original structure had no lobby, elevator, or ramp access for the handicapped and so required all of these plus theatrical rigging and lighting.

A newly designed addition provided a lobby with glass-block walls at the height of the building and two concrete towers housing an elevator and a stairwell. The fiberglass discs on top of the towers echo the adjacent structure remaining from the 1964 Fair.

Continued

1

2

78

1   Exterior
2   Exterior at night
3   Larger theater

3

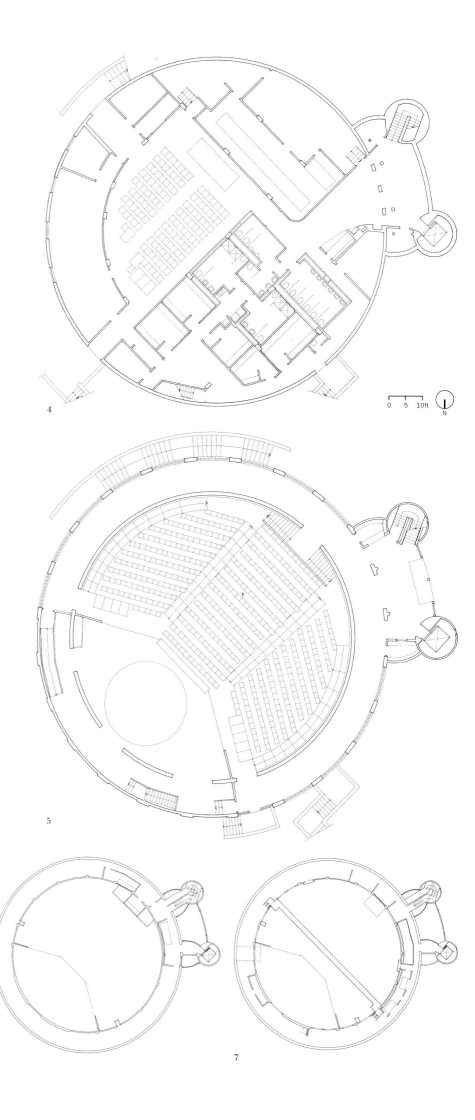

The existing structure was capped with an aluminum geodesic dome, permitting the use of the original wood dome for acoustical reflections and the support of theatrical rigging and lighting. The space between the two domes was insulated to protect the theater from nearby airport noise.

For economy's sake, old movie house seats were reconditioned for the larger, 500-seat theater on the main level. The 100-seat theater downstairs was planned for cabaret use and can be adapted to a variety of seating arrangements.

Paths to the theater and plaza at the entry were designed and landscaped according to the New York City Parks Department's master plan.

4

0   5   10ft

N

5

6

7

4   Plan of lower level
5   Plan of main level
6   Plan of first mezzanine
7   Plan of second mezzanine
8   Smaller theater
9   View of lobby looking up

8

9

The Diller-Quaile School of Music

Design/Completion 1996/1998
New York, New York
The Diller-Quaile School of Music
14,612 square feet (total project)
Steel stud with exterior insulating finishing system, flat roofs, wood joists
combined with steel, multiple layers of sheetrock on spring clips to
provide acoustical separation, hardwood and carpeted floor, renovated
masonry exterior wall

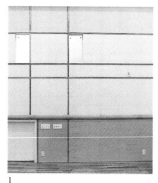

1

The Diller-Quaile School of Music accepts students of all ages but has been particularly successful working with very young children. To be able to expand and meet the demand for new classes, the school purchased an adjacent townhouse.

The design program for the new building included the addition of an elevator, fire stairs, new studios and office space, and a performance space to accommodate 99 people. The performance space will be used to showcase the skills of Diller-Quaile faculty and students and will also be available for community use.

The architects devised a structural system which allowed the performance space to be constructed without disrupting normal school activities. Acoustical requirements were given primary consideration when developing this space, and the floor was constructed with some flexibility to enhance dance performance.

On the front of the main building, a new ramp facilitates entry by the handicapped and ties into the historic landmarked facade.

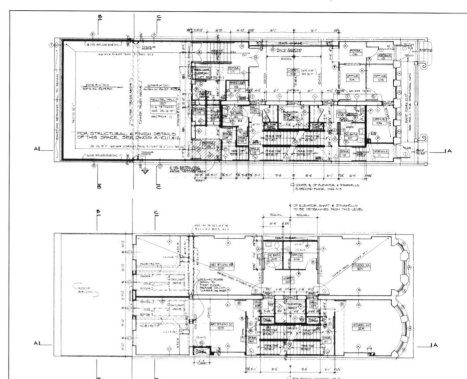

2

3

4

5

6

7

1   Rear wall of performance space
2   Working drawings
3   Front of building
4   Studio
5–7 Performance space

Stephen Gaynor School

Design/Completion 1993/1994
New York, New York
The Stephen Gaynor School
2,600 square feet
Steel studs and joists on existing structure, sheetrock, wood gym floor,
reinforced fiberglass windows, EIFS exterior finish, built-in work areas

This addition provided a multi-purpose activity room for a small private school for children with learning disabilities. In addition to conventional indoor sports facilities, the design incorporates work carrels for use by individual students.

Other renovations were accomplished within the structure of what had once been a West Side townhouse.

1

2

1   Landmarked exterior
2   Addition at rear
3   Interior
4   Work carrels
5   Exterior

3

4

5

The Allen-Stevenson School

Design/Completion 1993/1994
New York, New York
The Allen-Stevenson School
15,150 square feet
Concrete block bearing walls on concrete foundation; lightweight steel joists topped with steel deck and concrete; long-span steel joists over gym space; sheetrock walls over steel studs; fiberglass skylights

This project is an infill addition to two turn-of-the-century buildings owned by the Allen-Stevenson School in Manhattan. The school, which had an enrollment of 350 boys, occupied two buildings on 78th Street and two more on 77th Street. It was cramped for space and needed additional classrooms and a gymnasium.

On 77th Street, a five-story building was used for faculty housing and an adjacent lower building housed classroom space. The architects proposed to add three stories to the lower building and then place a gym over both buildings. The design of the addition vertically extends the piers of the existing building, while the use of brick and cut stone medallions at the top of the piers recalls similar elements on the building below. A new cornice line is established to match that of the adjacent five-story building.

The gym continues up past the cornice line. It is clad in metal to identify it as a separate structure, and thus maintains the scale of the two brick buildings.

The gym is set back in accordance with building regulations and is designed with opaque skylights to be light and bright without casting shadows on the courts.

1

2

3

4

5

1   Exterior
2   Locker room
3–5   Interior views of gym
6   Gym level plan
7   Music floor plan
8   Ground floor plan

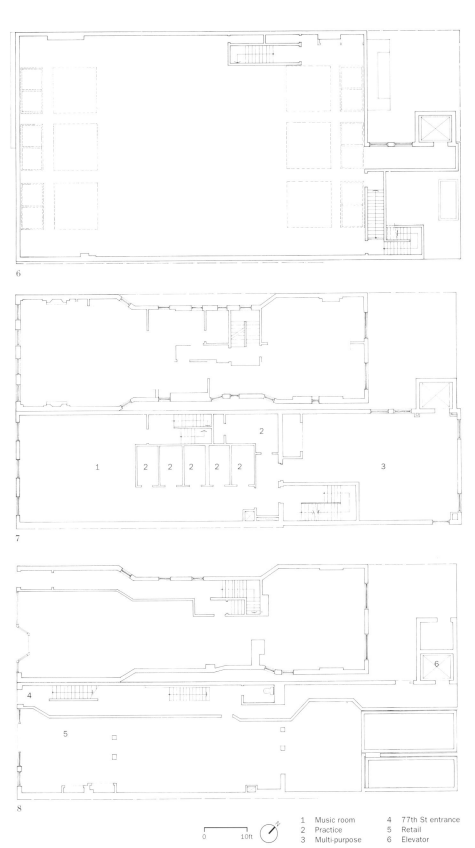

6

7

8

1   Music room   4   77th St entrance
2   Practice   5   Retail
3   Multi-purpose   6   Elevator

0   10ft

Chapel of Mt St Dominic

Design/Completion 1988/1989
Caldwell, New Jersey
Dominican Sisters of Mt St Dominic
4,860 square feet
Clear glass windows, stucco walls on original plaster, custom liturgical appointments

The Chapel of Mt St Dominic was built in 1983 for cloistered nuns of the Dominican Order. The atmosphere of the chapel—dark stained-glass windows and a remote altar—symbolized the withdrawal of the Sisters from the world. The renovation was designed to symbolize and enhance new liturgical concepts of worship.

In the new design, the altar is placed close to the congregation and the original sanctuary has been transformed by a low, curved wall into a small space for private prayer and meditation. Window frames have been opened almost to floor level to accommodate 37-foot-high clear glass windows, admitting natural light to the space.

A variety of seating arrangements are possible. All liturgical appointments were designed by the architects jointly with a team of artists from the religious community.

1

2

3

1–3　Renovated chapel interior
4　Exterior of chapel

4

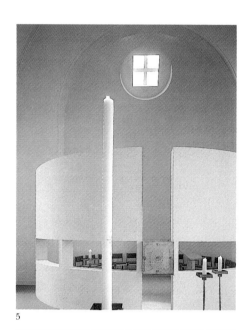

5

6

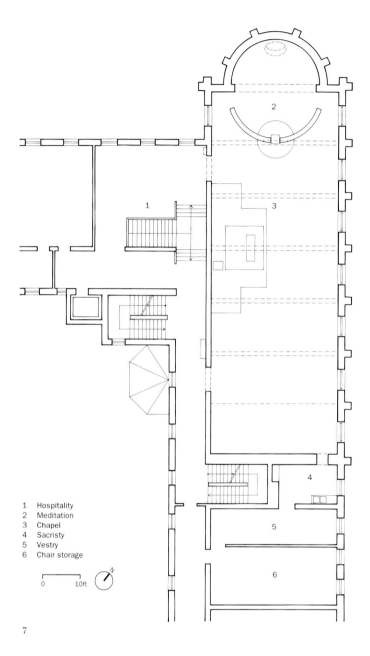

1   Hospitality
2   Meditation
3   Chapel
4   Sacristy
5   Vestry
6   Chair storage

0   10ft

7

5   Detail of apsidal chapel
6   Architect-designed liturgical furnishings
7   Plan
8   Interior

8

Community Church of Astoria

Design/Completion 1986/1987
Astoria, Queens, New York
Community Church of Astoria
4,000 square feet (addition); 2,000 square feet (renovation)
Textured and glazed concrete block, fiberglass, double-wall windows
and fixed panels, architect-designed chandeliers from electrical tubing
and stock fittings, sheetrock

The congregation of the Community Church of Astoria wanted to double the building's space at the same time as providing a multi-purpose room for meeting and Sunday School use.

To minimize disruption to church services and other activities during the construction process, the architects proposed building the new spaces above and to the side of the existing single-story church, effectively enveloping the older building. No demolition occurred until the new walls and roof were in place. This allowed the church to continue functioning for six months longer than if the original building had been demolished at the outset.

The exterior walls are a combination of split and ground-face concrete block in gray tones with red accent pieces. The pattern emphasizes the building's religious purposes.

1

2

1 Exterior side
2 Exterior front
3 Exterior
4 Exterior detail

3

4

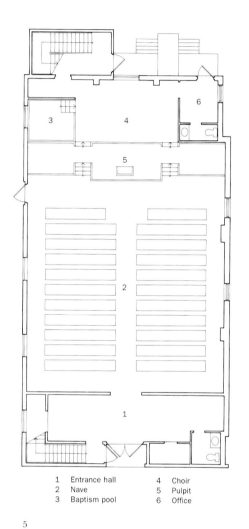

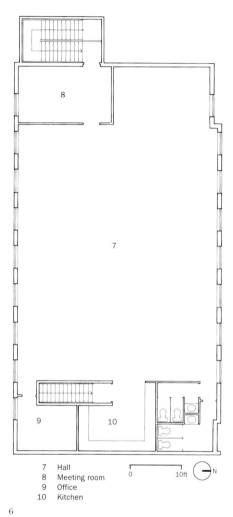

1	Entrance hall	4	Choir
2	Nave	5	Pulpit
3	Baptism pool	6	Office

7	Hall	
8	Meeting room	
9	Office	
10	Kitchen	

0   10ft   N

5

6

5 Church level plan
6 Meeting room (upper level) plan
7 Interior

7

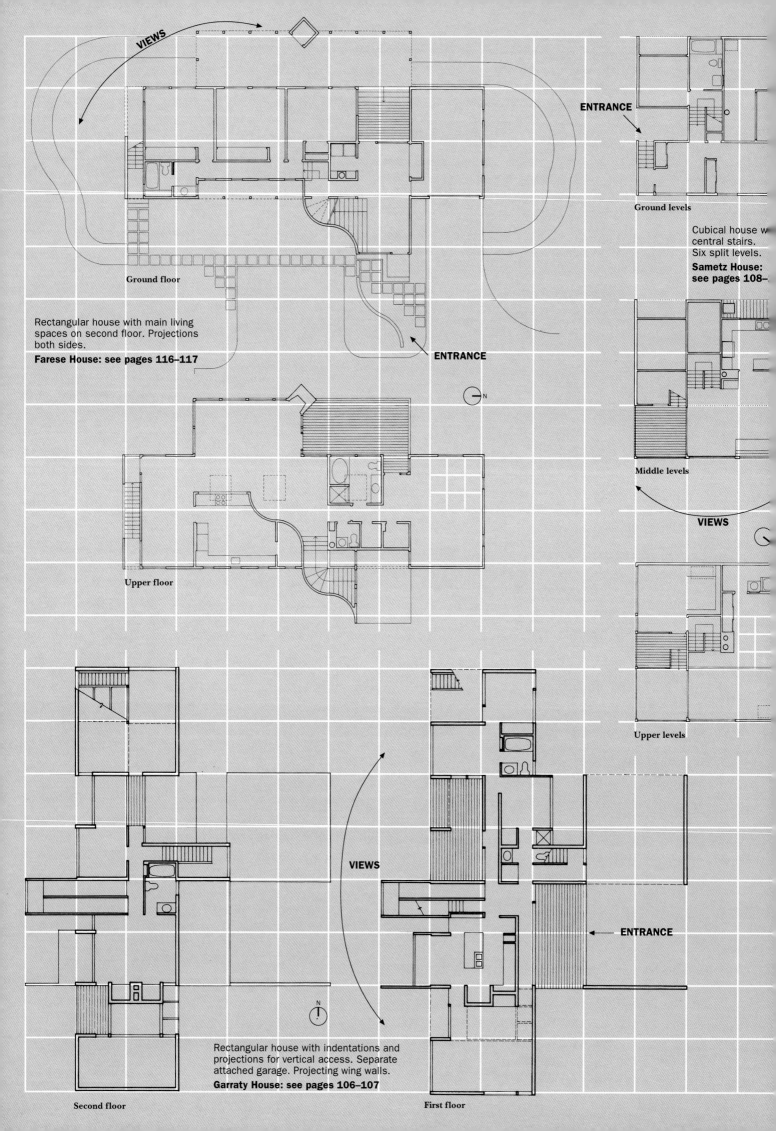

VIEWS

Ground floor

Rectangular house with main living
spaces on second floor. Projections
both sides.
Farese House: see pages 116–117

ENTRANCE

Upper floor

N

ENTRANCE

Ground levels

Cubical house w
central stairs.
Six split levels.
**Sametz House:
see pages 108–**

Middle levels

VIEWS

Upper levels

VIEWS

ENTRANCE

Second floor

N

Rectangular house with indentations and
projections for vertical access. Separate
attached garage. Projecting wing walls.
Garraty House: see pages 106–107

First floor

Shelter

Plans show the orientation of the shelter spaces to view, weather, and site features. They also show relationships between spaces within and the relative importance of those spaces to the program and client. All plans on these pages and the following project pages are at the same scale. Refer to the module key on this page.

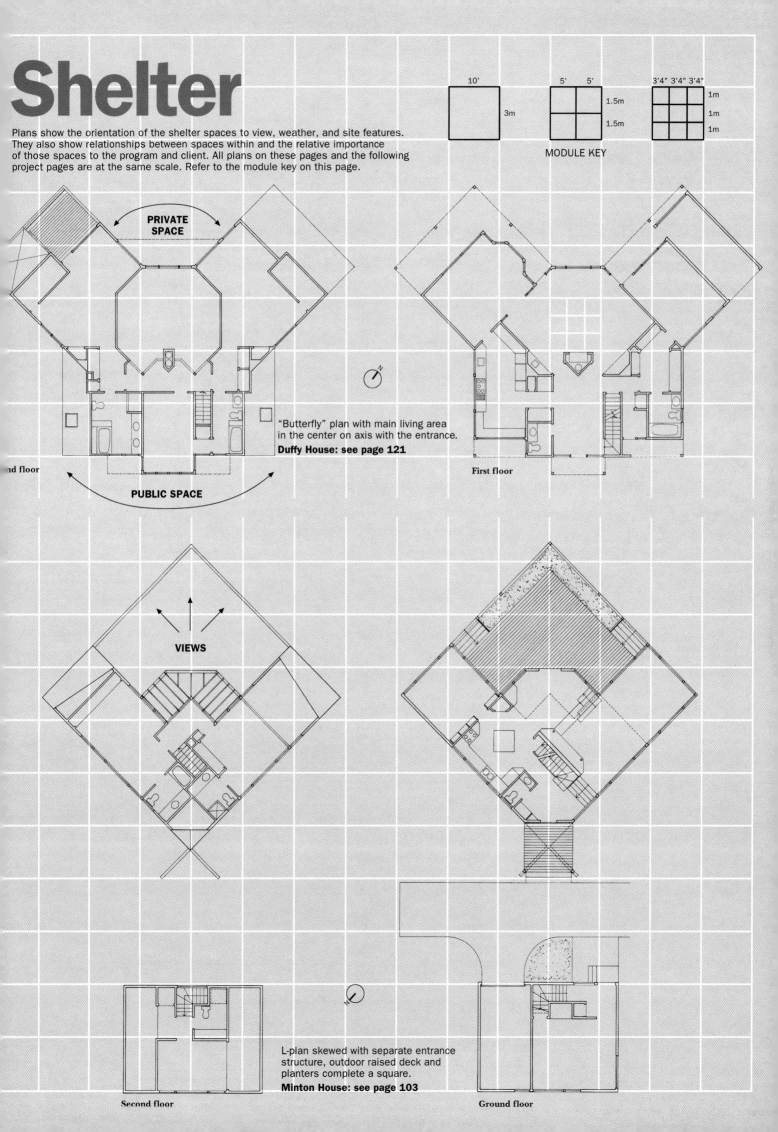

MODULE KEY

10'
3m

5' 5'
1.5m
1.5m

3'4" 3'4" 3'4"
1m
1m
1m

PRIVATE SPACE

PUBLIC SPACE

nd floor

"Butterfly" plan with main living area in the center on axis with the entrance.
Duffy House: see page 121

First floor

VIEWS

Second floor

L-plan skewed with separate entrance structure, outdoor raised deck and planters complete a square.
Minton House: see page 103

Ground floor

Moore House

Design/Completion 1987/1990
Connecticut
Client/Design collaborator: Richard & Noriko Moore
2,400 square feet (site area: 5 acres)
Wood structure cut from site oak trees; concrete retaining
walls, sand blasted or covered with stone; stone flooring;
wood sheathing or sheetrock (interior)

The main goal of the owners and architect was to merge this house into its natural environment. The site was selected so that the land would be minimally disturbed. The house was to face south toward a pond developed by the owners and was to fit within the landscape in a manner that provided no exposure to the north. Passive solar design controls the flow of energy through the building by natural means, utilizing energy conservation principles.

Some of the materials used were found on the site itself. Mature red oak trees on the property were selectively cut to provide posts and beams for the house. This was done long enough before ground breaking to ensure that the lumber was aged. Old fieldstone walls on the property provided material for facing the concrete walls. The main building materials are concrete (sand-blasted in some areas, and faced with stone in others) and oak posts and beams.

An important design consideration was the proportion of the walls with the glass areas. Natural light is brought into the rear of the house via a long row of skylights and even on an overcast day, one does not feel "underground" in any room. The rich colorings of the wood, stone, and other materials further distance any feeling of subterranean space.

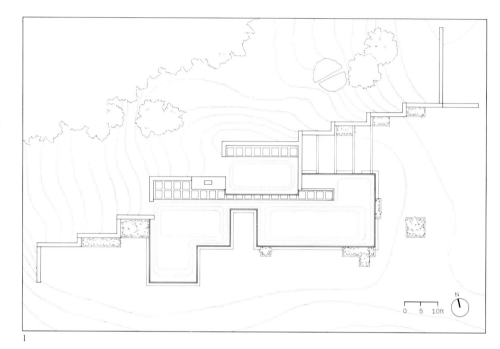

1

2

96

1 Site plan
2 View across pond
3 Entrance court
4 Exterior
5 View from the southeast

3

4

5

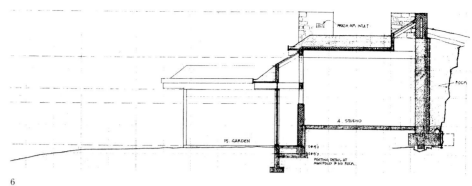

6

6   Section through studio
7   Screened porch
8   Elevations
9   Floor plan
10   Central corridor looking toward dining room
11   Living room
12   Window detail
13   Fireplace in living room
14   Bedroom

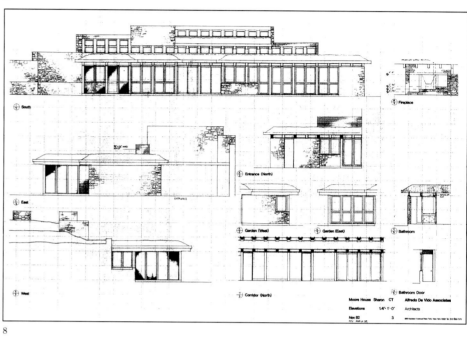

7

8

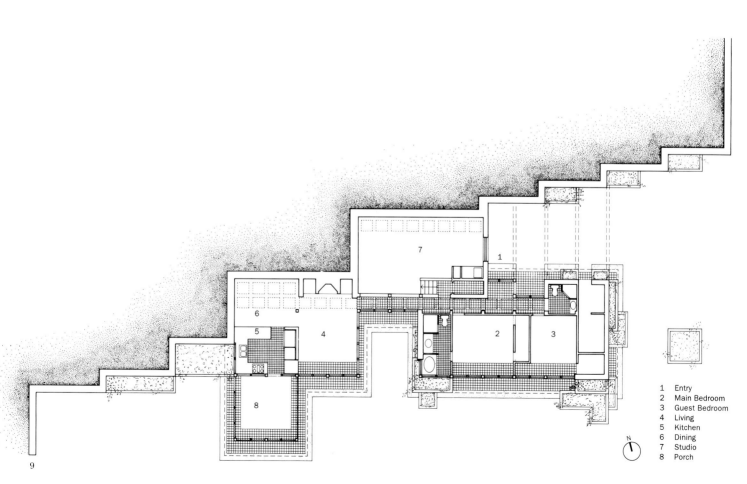

1   Entry
2   Main Bedroom
3   Guest Bedroom
4   Living
5   Kitchen
6   Dining
7   Studio
8   Porch

9

11

12

13

10

14

Wirth House

Design/Completion 1974/1975
Waccabuc, New York
Willard and Marnee Wirth
2,300 square feet (site area: 2 acres)
Wood frame, concrete footings and retaining walls
Horizontal cedar boards, wood windows, stone facing
for retaining walls and chimney

The rooms of this three-level house were arranged side by side in response to the shape of the site, and in order to gain winter sun exposure and summer cross-ventilation for all rooms. Because of this arrangement of rooms, the house projects an appearance of great size toward the steep driveway, which is lined with maple and tulip trees.

Entry is at the lower level. A flight of stairs leads to the dining room and kitchen, and a few more steps to the compact living room, with windows looking south, east, and west. Another flight of stairs leads to a study above the kitchen.

Cedar boards on the walls and floors combine with a tall fieldstone fireplace to provide an aura of solid comfort.

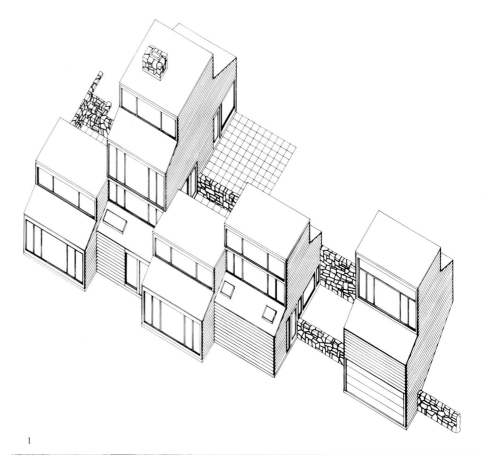

1

2

1 Axonometric
2 Downhill side of house towards view
3 Site plan
4 Sketch of living room
5 View from approach
6 View from front
7 Living room

3

0   40ft   N

5

6

4

7

8   Bathroom
9   Play room
10   Living room seating area
11   Upper level floor plan
12   Lower level floor plan
13   Dining/kitchen

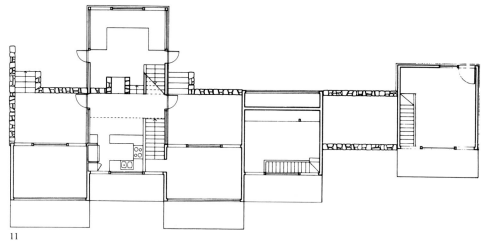

11

8

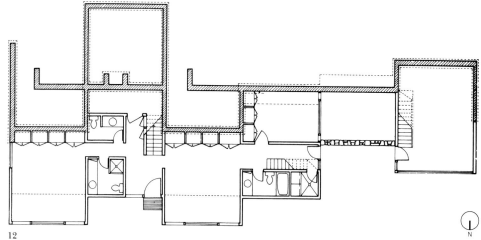

12

9

10

13

Minton House

Design/Completion 1982/1983
Copake, New York
Stuart and Debbie Minton
2,020 square feet (house), 920 square feet (guest house)
(site area: 20 acres)
Wood frame
Vertical stained cedar boards (interior and exterior), stone fireplace,
stenciled pine flooring, sheetrock, aluminum thermal windows

The clients for this country house wanted
to have a flower garden close to the house.
To protect the garden from hungry deer
and rabbits, the architects provided a
raised, enclosed garden court, open to
the birch forest on two sides and flanked
by the house on the other two. Rooms
look through the garden court to the
forest beyond.

In the living room and adjacent dining
area, the natural cedar boards are
whitewashed. The wide pineboard floors
are stenciled with a pattern, adding
richness to an otherwise simple range
of materials.

1   Raised garden
2   Plan
3   Dining area
4   Living room
5   Exterior at dusk

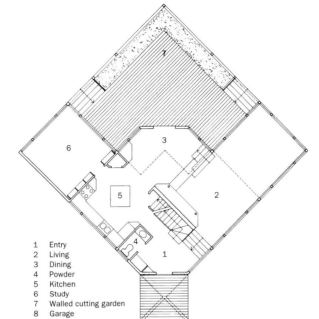

1   Entry
2   Living
3   Dining
4   Powder
5   Kitchen
6   Study
7   Walled cutting garden
8   Garage

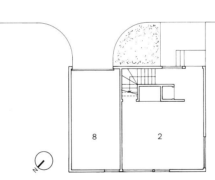

Sheehy House

Design/Completion 1972/1973
East Hampton, New York
John and Morna Sheehy
2,000 square feet (site area: 1 acre)
Wood frame, concrete foundations
Horizontal stained cedar siding (exterior), unfinished cedar siding
(interior), tile and wood floors, stucco fireplace

Sited on an inside lot of a wooded
subdivision, the long, narrow house
is made up of two kinds of spaces, or
"zones," to accommodate the family
of five. At one end are the children's
bedrooms and play spaces; at the other
end are the main living room, the master
bedroom, and the other family areas.
The long side on the north faces the
access drive, from which one may enter
directly either the family or the children's
wing. The two spaces are connected at the
second story by an enclosed bridge.

The focus of the house is the two-story
living room, with its liberal windows that
open it up on three sides to views of the
natural woodland. The entrance, dining
areas, and even the master bedroom open
onto this room, each "borrowing" from
the other's space to extend the apparent
size of this modestly proportioned house.

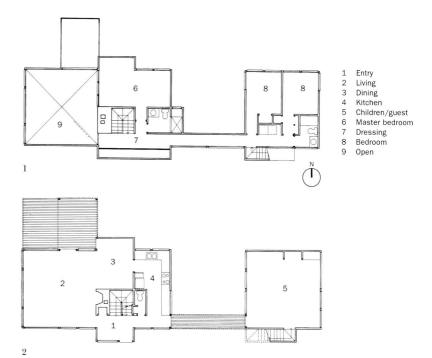

1   Entry
2   Living
3   Dining
4   Kitchen
5   Children/guest
6   Master bedroom
7   Dressing
8   Bedroom
9   Open

1

2

3

4

1   Upper level plan
2   Lower level plan
3   Entrance
4   Addition to house
5   Front of house
6   Back of house
7   Deck/exterior living
8&9   Living room
10   Master bedroom
11   Front entrance
12   Kitchen

5

6

7

8

9

10

11

12

Garraty House

Design/Completion 1972/1973
Sag Harbor, New York
Jack and Gail Garraty
2,300 square feet (site area: 1.5 acres)
Concrete block bearing walls on concrete foundation, infill with wood frame
Concrete block waterproofed on outside with thick paste waterproofing over struck joints; painted steel trowel concrete floors; flat roof

Designed to economically fulfill the client's desire for a masonry house and to withstand attack from wind-blown sand and rain, this bayfront house is built of waterproofed concrete block. The block has been filled with insulation to provide good thermal barriers.

The house is divided into a living level, a quiet level, and a roof solarium. The owner's main living areas are on the lowest level, with floors of concrete softened by throw rugs and duck boards. The second level rooms are for retiring; the finishes are softer—mostly carpet and wood. The artist's studio has two skylights arranged to catch good diffuse northern light. There is also a two-bedroom guest apartment.

The elongated plan provides every room with a view west toward Peconic Bay and with the comforts of cross-ventilation. Overhung porches and recesses protect the rooms from the western sun.

1

2

3

4

1 Front of house
2 End of house
3 Model
4 Living room
5 Second floor plan
6 Lower level plan
7 Kitchen
8 Vehicular approach
9 Bay side of house

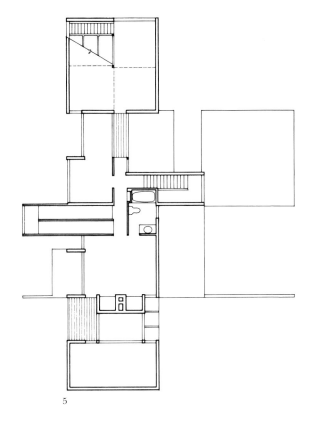

5

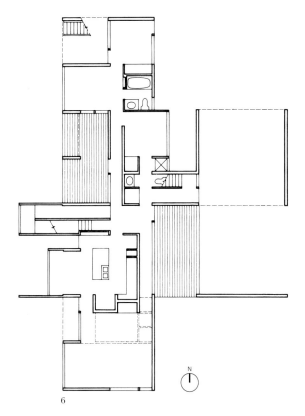

6

N

7

8

9

Sametz House

Design/Completion 1979/1980
Garrison, New York
Arnold and Agnes Sametz
Site area: 2 acres
Wood frame, vertical stained wood cedar siding, sheetrock
interior, hardwood floors, built-up composition roof

This 30 feet by 30 feet cubical house is made up of interlocked levels, all of which have splendid views of the Hudson River.

Because of its simple shape, the house was economical to build. Other facilitating factors were the utilization of the architect's design module, condensed drawings, and typical construction details. The shape also makes it easy to heat and cool the house, since it exposes limited surface area to the elements. Cedar boards, stained black to set the house off quietly in the landscape, also serve to absorb additional heat in winter. Deciduous trees shade the surface in summer.

The apparent size of the relatively small house, and of the spaces within it, is extended through various spatial devices, including the placement of windows to bring light in from unexpected sources, such as clerestories and skylights.

Living areas include a master bedroom remote from two others for visiting children, with a living/dining area occupying the center of the house.

1

2

3

1   Axonometric
2   Exterior
3   View from porch
4   Entry/bedroom level plan
5   Living/kitchen level plan
6   Master bedroom level plan
7   Living room from dining area
8   Living room
9   Kitchen
10   Fireplace
11   Library
12   Master bedroom

4

1   Vestibule
2   Bedroom
3   Study/
    Bedroom
4   Bath
5   Open to below

7

8

5

1   Living
2   Kitchen
3   Deck

9

10

6

1   Master
    Bedroom
2   Bath
3   Library
4   Deck
5   Open to below

11

12

West House

Design/Completion 1972/1973
East Hampton, New York
Paul West
1,500 square feet (site area: 1 acre)
Wood frame, concrete foundation
Cedar shingles (exterior), cedar boards (interior), tile and wood floors

The program called for a tightly organized house of two stories, which would intrude as little as possible on the surrounding natural landscape. The design organizes the elements on the diagonal of a square, with bedrooms and smaller spaces on one side and a tall living/dining space on the other.

The spaces are grouped around the chimney mass, the symbolic center of the house. The concept is reflected on the exterior, where the roofs are pitched inward and down to permit glazing on the exterior walls to catch views, light, and air.

1

1   Exterior from entrance side
2   Exterior from garden
3   Dining area
4   Detail
5   Living area
6   Rear section
7   Lower level plan
8   Upper level plan

2

3

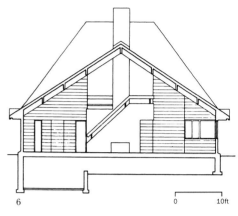

6

0   10ft

4

5

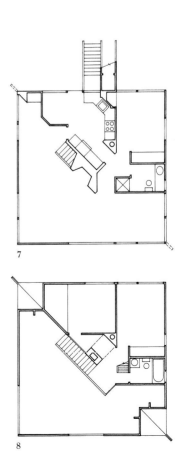

7

8

Wertheimer House

Design/Completion 1983/1984
Bethany Beach, Delaware
Loretta and Richard Wertheimer
2,500 square feet (site area: 0.25 acre)
Wood frame raised on treated piles for flood purposes, stained cedar boards, whitewashed cedar plywood paneling

This octagonal house was designed to serve as a weekend/vacation retreat for a Washington, DC attorney and his family (six in all). It is located in Bethany Beach, a seaside resort with high density zoning. Since neighboring houses blocked the direct ocean view, the major spaces were oriented to catch an oblique glimpse of dunes and sea.

Because of the proximity to the ocean, Federal Flood Insurance rules required the house to be set on pilings, with the lowest living floor above high tide level. To avoid the awkwardness of a house on stilts, the lower level pilings were surrounded with textured cedar plywood. This was acceptable under the regulation governing stories below flood tide level, and the room serves well as overflow space on busy weekends.

Continued

1

1 Sketch
2 View from the ocean
3 View from the land
4 View from the screened porch

2

3

The textured plywood covering the lower level of the house is stained black to emphasize its purpose as the house's base. The landscaping is mounded around it in dune fashion and planted with indigenous vegetation. Upper levels of the house are clad in "weatherboard," a locally used cedar bevel siding, stained gray.

Internal spaces are organized around the large, high-ceilinged living area which features freestanding columns and a series of exposed beams for lateral bracing. Interior surfaces are clad in rough-cut cedar plywood panels, whitewashed to eliminate color variance.

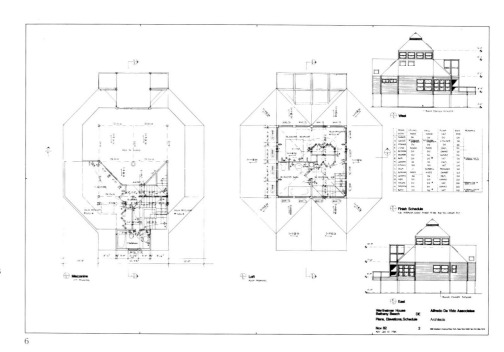

6

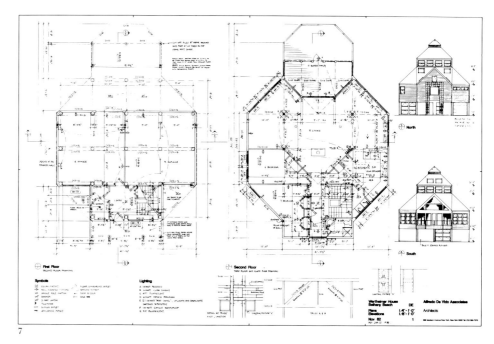

7

5

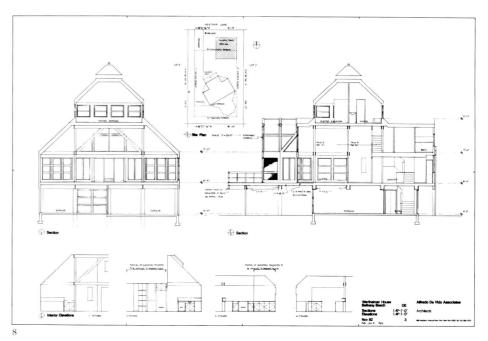

8

9

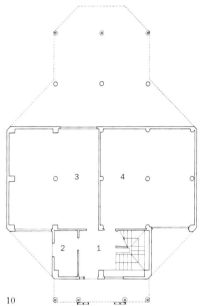
10

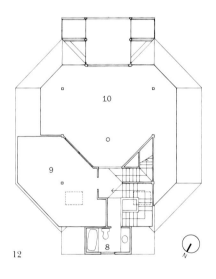
12

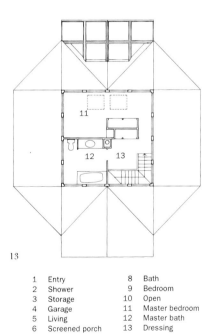
11

14

15

16

13

N

1	Entry	8	Bath
2	Shower	9	Bedroom
3	Storage	10	Open
4	Garage	11	Master bedroom
5	Living	12	Master bath
6	Screened porch	13	Dressing
7	Kitchen		

5	House at dusk
6–8	Working drawings
9	Lighting detail
10	First floor plan
11	Second floor plan
12	Mezzanine plan
13	Loft plan
14	Kitchen
15	Dining area
16	Master bedroom

Farese House

Design/Completion 1988/1988
Montauk, New York
Carmine and Carol Farese
Interior Designer: Catherine De Vido
2,360 square feet (house), 200 square feet (garage) (site area: 2 acres)
Wood frame, concrete foundation
Vertical cedar siding, painted sheetrock, aluminum thermal windows,
tile kitchen and baths

An assessment of the site showed that trees on a nearby property would completely obscure views from the ground floor level of the house. The design therefore raised the living areas and master bedroom to the second floor level, which is reached from the entry by a wide, curving staircase. From the top of the stair there are commanding views of Gardiner's Bay.

The interior wall planes are defined in soft pastel colors.

1

1   View showing stair cutout
2   Side view
3   Lower level plan
4   Upper level plan
5   Kitchen from living room
6   Stair to second floor
7   Master bedroom

2

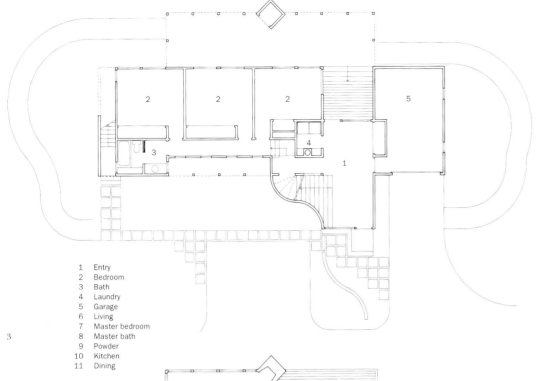

1. Entry
2. Bedroom
3. Bath
4. Laundry
5. Garage
6. Living
7. Master bedroom
8. Master bath
9. Powder
10. Kitchen
11. Dining

3

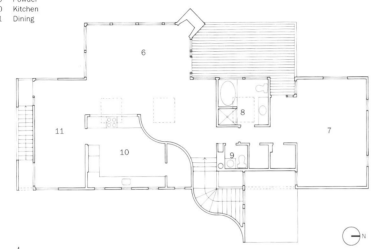

4

6

5

7

Matthews House

Design/Completion 1966/1967
East Hampton, New York
Hale Matthews
2,000 square feet (site area: 1 acre)
Wood frame
Cedar shingle cladding (exterior), natural cypress board cladding (interior),
Mexican tile floors

Views, protection from occasional high winds, comfort, low maintenance, and space for weekend guests—these were the chief requirements for this house on an exposed site on the eastern end of Long Island.

The two-story living space is divided into active and quiet areas by the tall brick fireplace and stairs that lead to the upper bedroom. The dining area looks south toward a cool stand of trees. Concealed clerestory windows have been used around the top of the fireplace, allowing natural daylight to filter into the living room. Materials are natural and easy to maintain: rough-cut cypress boards for the walls and kitchen cabinets, and tile for the floors.

Bordering the house on three sides is a deck of spruce planks. A path and steep flight of steps connect the house with the seashore 30 feet below.

1

1–3 Exterior views
   4 Living room
   5 Lower level plan
   6 Upper level plan
   7 Porch in upper level
   8 Detail
   9 View from stair to below

2

3

118

4

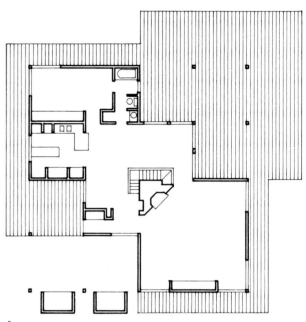

5

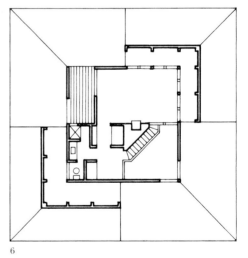

6

7

8

9

10

11

12

13

10   Living room
11   Detail
12   Porch side of living room
13   Kitchen

Duffy House

Design/Completion 1990/1991
Wainscott, New York
Vincent and Vivi Duffy
2,800 square feet (site area: 0.5 acre)
Wood frame
Vertical cedar boards, fiberglass shingles on roof, painted sheetrock interior, tile baths, carpeted floors

The location of this property—near ocean beaches and overlooking handsome landscaped grounds—was appealing, but neighboring houses gave it little privacy. To counter this problem, the architects designed a house plan shaped like a butterfly, with wings extending diagonally toward the rear of the property. From within the house, views of adjacent homes are blocked and focus is directed to the garden and swimming pool. Fences extending from the wings further control the view and afford privacy for outdoor living.

The center of the house is occupied by a two-story octagonal living room, which faces the garden. The skewed wings contain a guest room on one side and the kitchen and dining room on the other. Two bedrooms on the second floor, oriented toward the south-facing garden, are separated by a study.

The interior is detailed with a pattern of wood moldings, harmonizing with the owner's collection of antiques.

1   Entry
2   Living
3   Dining
4   Guest
5   Garage
6   Laundry

1   Lower level plan
2   Living room
3   Front of house

2

3

De Vido House

Design/Completion 1968/1997
East Hampton, New York
Alfredo and Catherine De Vido
2,300 square feet (house), 600 square feet (studio), 600 square feet
(garage) (site area: 2 acres)
Composite wood post and girt
Cedar shingles stained gray (exterior), rough-cut cedar boards (interior),
natural and stained pine floors, wood shingle roofs

The project has been an ongoing series of additions using wood as the primary building material. The basic house, completed in 1968, was 1,200 square feet. A prime structural element of the house is a large wood X truss supporting a 5-foot cantilever. Sunlight filtering from windows and skylights into the wood-lined rooms creates a warm and glowing atmosphere.

Recent additions include a vestibule on the front facade, two bedrooms and an expanded kitchen in the rear, and various garden structures in the landscape. The additions recall the forms of the existing house and are executed in the same vocabulary of wood detailing.

1

2

3

1–3 Exterior views of house at various stages
4 Dining room from living room
5 Studio building interior
6 Master bedroom
7 Exterior landscape

4

5

6

7

8   Interior of house from second floor
9   First floor of house as initially built
10 Second floor of house as initially built
11 Gazebo across pool
12 Exterior before water feature was built
13 First floor with addition
14 Second floor with addition
15 Second floor alcove
16 Vestibule
17 Living room

8

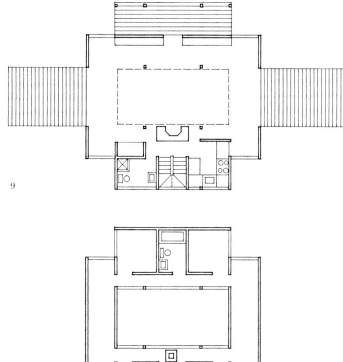

9

10

11

12

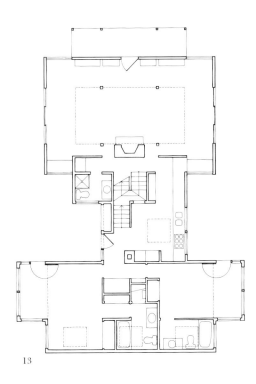

13

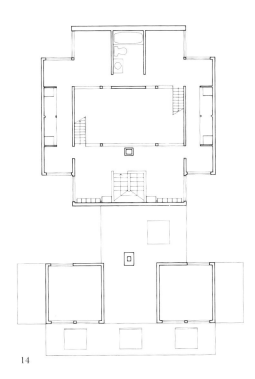

14

15

16

17

18

18 Studio building
19 Exterior
20 Pond

19

20

Ross House

Design/Completion 1960/1961
East Hampton, New York
Hal Ross
3,200 square feet (site area: 2 acres)
Wood frame reinforced with steel collar to resist hurricane winds
Stained cedar shingle cladding (exterior), sheetrock (interior), stone
fireplace, tile and hardwood floors

Set behind a dune facing the Atlantic
Ocean, this house recalls early American
"salt-box" forms in its shape and detailing.
The main room is two stories high and
around it are clustered the secondary
living spaces. Large plate glass windows
are protected by a deep overhang and
lateral sunshades to avoid excessive heat
buildup from the strong southerly sun.
Space flows freely from one room to
another in this plan.

1   Living room
2&3   Exterior views

1

2

3

3 White Pine Road

Design/Completion 1985/1986
East Hampton, New York
2,750 square feet (house), 200 square feet (garage) (site area: 2 acres)
Wood frame
Cedar shingle cladding (exterior), painted sheetrock (interior), natural
pine floors

In 1976, the architect subdivided a 35-acre parcel of land in East Hampton, New York. Since then, he has built for sale seven houses on the property.

This is one of the later houses in the series; like the others, it is sited for privacy, views, and solar orientation, and makes use of the natural wood shingles and painted wood trim which have been used on eastern Long Island since the 1600s. These materials have proven durable and give a certain distinction to the landscape.

The gabled roof recalls earlier houses of the area; however, the architect sought a contemporary expression through the use of large expanses of glass, the placement of windows, and the inclusion of skew walls and lofty, open rooms.

1

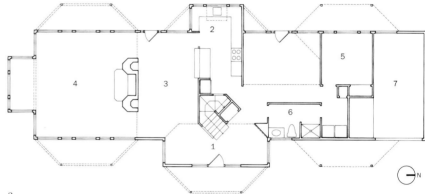

2

1 Rear of house
2 First floor plan
3 Rear of house at dusk
4 Second floor plan
5 Front elevation drawing
6 Front entrance
7&8 Living room
9 Entrance hall

3

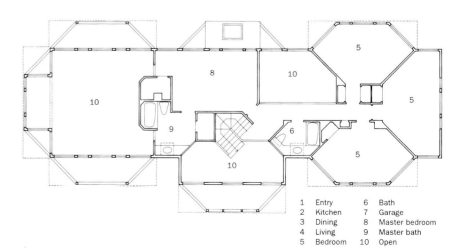

4

1	Entry	6	Bath
2	Kitchen	7	Garage
3	Dining	8	Master bedroom
4	Living	9	Master bath
5	Bedroom	10	Open

5

7

8

6

9

1 White Pine Road

Design/Completion 1986/1987
East Hampton, New York
2,970 square feet (site area: 2 acres)
Wood frame
Cedar shingles trimmed with painted wood, thermal aluminum windows,
fiberglass shingles, sheetrock interior walls, natural pine floors

This is another house in the White Pine Road series. Again, the aim is for a harmonious grouping: certain forms and materials are introduced and repeated, yet each house has its individual character.

This house is the eighth in the group and it has the triple gable, curving brackets, and cedar shingles found in other dwellings in the region. To unify and emphasize the house's various window openings and voids, distinctive bands of trim are painted dark green. Within the house, the shaping of space and detailing are contemporary. The plan permits two sets of stairs to bedrooms on each side of the living room, allowing greater flexibility of use and privacy in those areas.

1

2

1   Rear elevation drawing
2   Entrance
3   Front of house
4   Living room looking to rear
5   Living room
6   Rear of house
7   First floor plan
8   Second floor plan
9   Living room

3

4

5

130

6

7

8

9

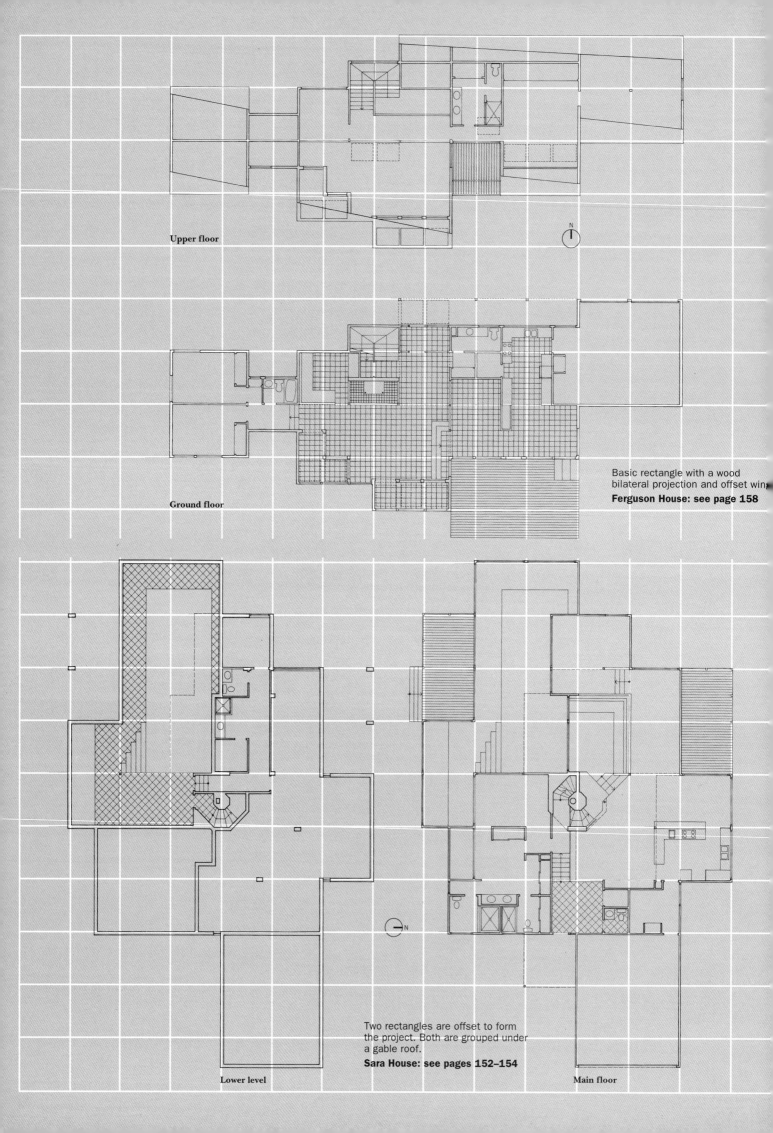

Upper floor

Ground floor

Basic rectangle with a wood
bilateral projection and offset wing.
Ferguson House: see page 158

Two rectangles are offset to form
the project. Both are grouped under
a gable roof.
Sara House: see pages 152–154

Lower level

Main floor

Shelter

Rectangular plans are generally more economical. Compact plans with central circulation cores can minimize circulation space and enable living spaces to face out to views and light. All plans on these pages and the following project pages are at the same scale. Refer to the module key on this page.

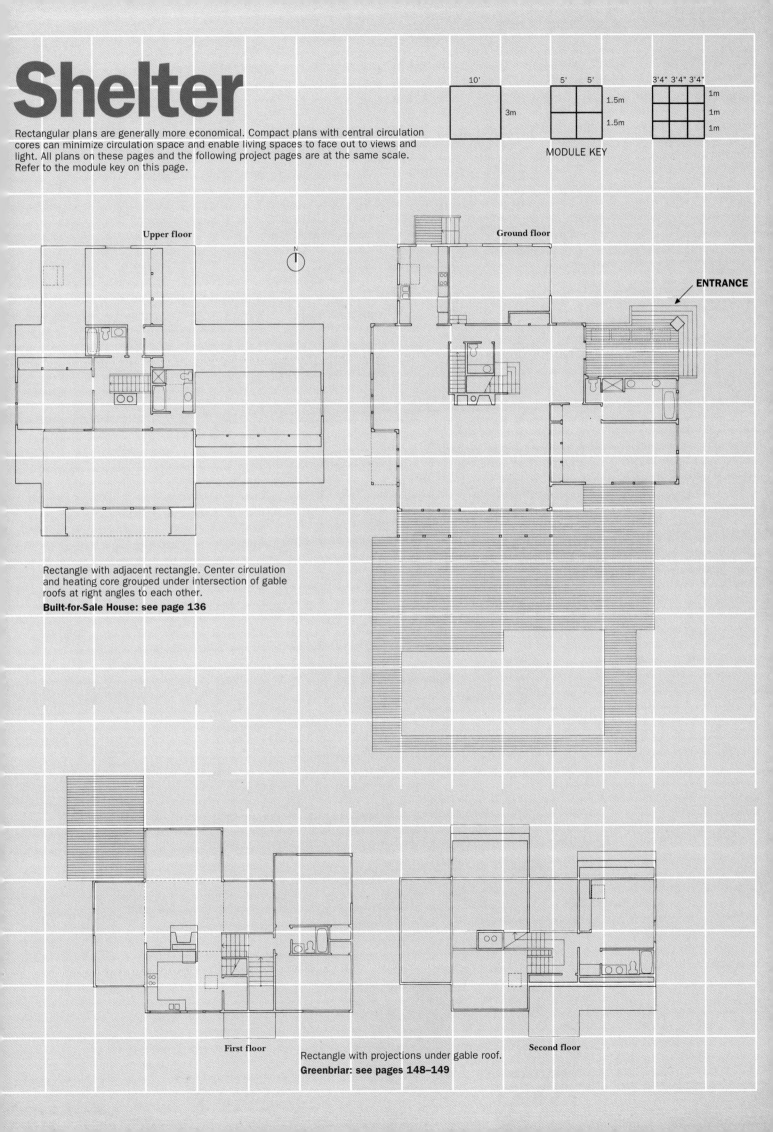

10'   3m

5' 5'   1.5m   1.5m

3'4" 3'4" 3'4"   1m   1m   1m

MODULE KEY

Upper floor

N

Ground floor

ENTRANCE

Rectangle with adjacent rectangle. Center circulation and heating core grouped under intersection of gable roofs at right angles to each other.

Built-for-Sale House: see page 136

First floor

Rectangle with projections under gable roof.

Greenbriar: see pages 148–149

Second floor

Hammer House

Design/Completion 1972/1973
Sagaponack, New York
Mr and Mrs Richard Hammer
2,000 square feet (site area: 1 acre)
Wood frame
Stained rough-cut cedar boards (interior and exterior), tile and wood
floors, stucco fireplace, wood deck

The site for this house was an open lot in
the corner of a potato field. The design
recognized this by clustering small shed
and gabled units around a large deck
open to the ocean view to the south,
and the setting sun to the west. Elevations
present largely closed facades to the roads
on the north and east, while skylights over
the kitchen provide light and expand the
space in that direction from the living
area.

The articulation of the plan into separate
units reflects the spatial organization and
also gives the relatively small house a
larger scale in the wide expanse of the
surrounding fields. Guests are
accommodated in a separate guest house.

The standard wood frame construction
is sheathed inside and out with rough-cut
cedar boards and the roof is exposed
plank and beam sheathed with wood
shingles.

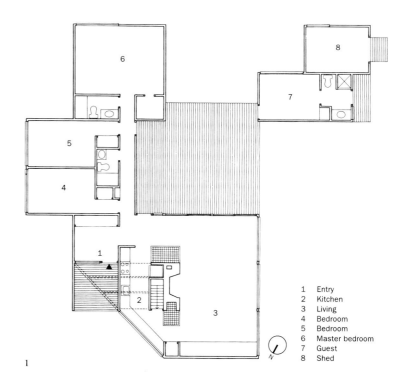

1

1   Entry
2   Kitchen
3   Living
4   Bedroom
5   Bedroom
6   Master bedroom
7   Guest
8   Shed

1   Plan
2   Court
3   Section
4   Court
5   Eating alcove
6&7   Living room

2

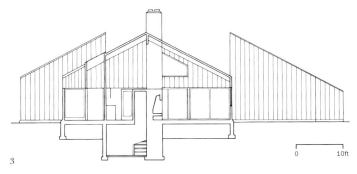

3

4

5

6

7

Built-for-Sale House

Design/Completion 1987/1988
East Hampton, New York
3,000 square feet (site area: 1 acre)
Wood frame
Cedar shingles, siding, and roof trimmed with printed wood; sheetrock
interior; hardwood and carpeted floors

On vacant land in a resort area, the
owners wanted to build a house for sale
that would appeal to a broad spectrum of
potential buyers. Among the features they
wanted incorporated in the house were:
a large master bedroom suite with skylight
over a sitting area; a large living room with
L-shaped dining area adjacent; a ground
floor bedroom open to the outside;
traditional shape and trim; a modern,
open kitchen with eat-in area; a pool and
large deck for outdoor dining; and natural
landscaping.

1

2

3

4

1   Rear of house
2   Entrance side
3   Detail
4   Living room

Goodman House

Design/Completion 1977/1978
Quogue, New York
Arthur and Betty Goodman
4,000 square feet (site area: 2 acres)
Wood frame on wood piles with concrete floor connection
Cedar boards (interior and exterior), cedar shingle roof

To conform with new regulations governing oceanfront buildings, the house had to be built on pilings and placed behind the primary sand dune. To preserve ocean views over the dune, secondary bedrooms and spaces were located on the lower level, where they make the most of the views over Shinnecock Bay to thc north. The master bedroom and living areas are on top, along with generous decks around the swimming pool. The living/dining area is open to the kitchen, which is designed to accommodate food preparation for large numbers of friends and family.

Another social area on the lower level provides for games and television viewing. A separate building houses changing facilities and some added living space for this large and close-knit family. The house is clad in cedar, which weathers well in the ocean climate. It is angled on the site to afford broad views of the ocean and bay.

1

2

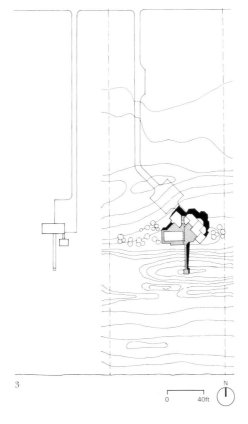

3

4

1 Beach side
2 Beach side by pool
3 Site plan
4 Detail

0   40ft   N

Fried House

Design/Completion 1977/1978
Amagansett, New York
Mr and Mrs Wilbur Fried
Landscape Design: Connelly/Hollander
Interior Furnishings: Lembo/Bohn
3,540 square feet (site area: 1 acre)

Plants growing on this duneland property signaled the presence of freshwater wetlands. Since land-use within 100 feet of certain wetlands is regulated by environmental conservation law, the owner was required to deed to the Town a scenic easement over much of the property. The buildable area was thus reduced to a small percentage of the site that adjoined neighboring houses.

For the sake of privacy, the design consists of a long gable roof with mostly blank end walls near neighboring houses. The plan affords all rooms a view of the sand dunes and ocean to the south. Glass areas are sheltered from the sun's glare by a deep overhang. On the street side, the shingled exterior is embellished with curved openings.

The living area is a flowing space 50 feet long, some of it double height, which overlooks a patio and large swimming pool. The pool has a curved retaining wall that follows the wetlands setback line. Landscaping around the pool harmonizes with the natural vegetation.

1

2

3

1 Rear of house overlooking bay view
2 Walkway over living room
3 Living room
4 Lower level plan
5 View from dining area to living area
6 Front elevation

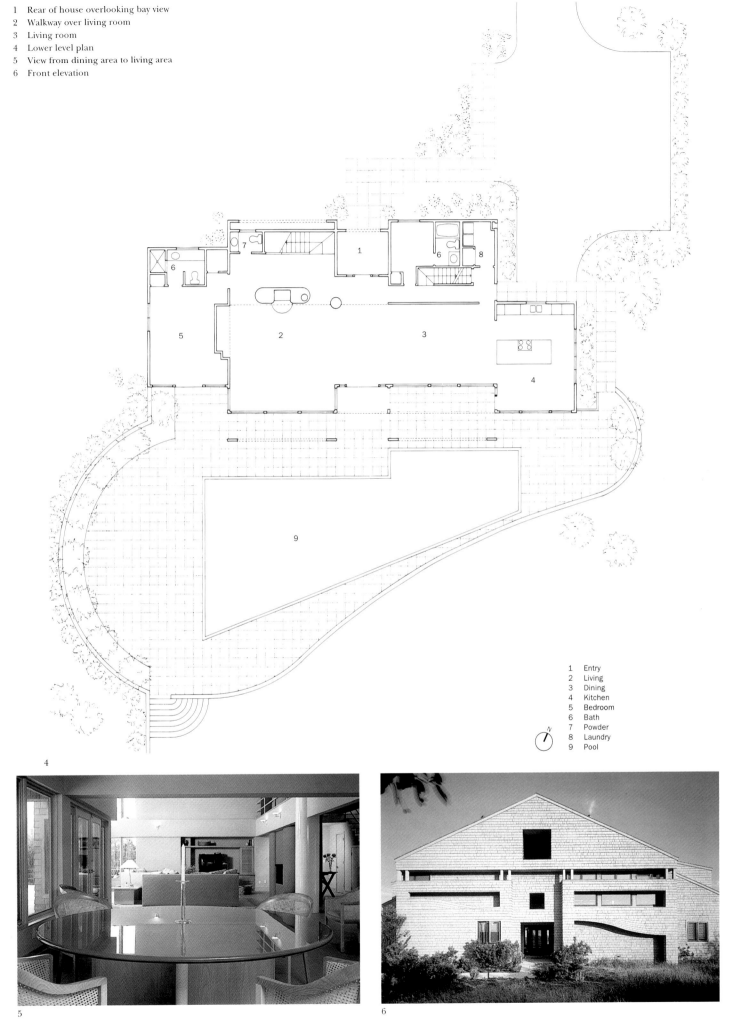

1 Entry
2 Living
3 Dining
4 Kitchen
5 Bedroom
6 Bath
7 Powder
8 Laundry
9 Pool

N

4

5   6

Snow King Inn

Design/Completion 1976/1978
Jackson, Wyoming
Snow King Inn
100 hotel rooms, conference facilities for 500 attendees, public areas (site area: 20 acres)
Wood, heavy timber truss construction, concrete foundation
Vertical cedar boards, cedar shake shingles, sheetrock and wood interior finishes, shaped concrete block interior fire walls

This hotel/motel/conference center is located at the edge of Jackson's residential area at the base of Snow King Mountain, a popular recreation spot. The owner wanted uninterrupted access to the mountain and required generous spaces for the building. The program called for a center with 100 guest rooms and supporting services, which could ultimately be expanded to accommodate 500 to 700 attendees.

The resulting scheme has buildings ranging from one to six stories, and tight internal circulation. The contours of the mountain and surrounding terrain helped shape the profiles of the medium-rise wing and connecting facilities. Each room has a striking view of the landscape.

The guest room wings are plank on block-bearing walls, with metal stud partitions and an exterior skin faced with natural cedar. The central facility is steel-framed with wood trusses to permit large spans and vertical spaces. Natural cedar was chosen for the exterior. The balconies and windows of the guest room wings give scale to the structure and link it to the architecture of the region.

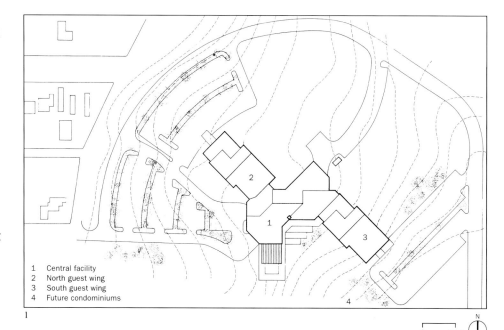

1   Central facility
2   North guest wing
3   South guest wing
4   Future condominiums

1

0   100ft   N

2

140

1   Site plan
2   View from the southwest
3&4   Buildings in the landscape

3

4

5

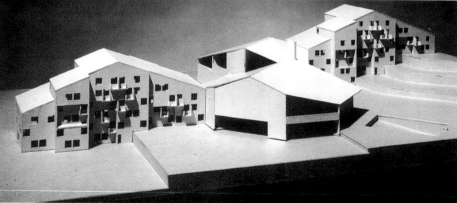

6

5   View from the north
6&7 Model studies
8   View from the west
9   View from the mountain in winter
10   View from the southwest in winter

7

8

9

10

11

12

13

11 Main room
12 Conference center
13 Lounge

Berkowitz Addition/Renovation

Design/Completion 1994/1995
Westhampton Beach, New York
Natalie and Phil Berkowitz
4,900 square feet (site area: 1 acre)
Existing walls, additional wood structure
Stained cedar shingles, wood exterior trim, aluminum thermal windows,
tiles, carpet

The original 1930s house had an ungainly appearance, partly due to a clumsy addition carried out some time after the original construction. The architects wanted to respect the spirit of the era and style of the house while sorting out design problems and adding necessary amenities.

The solution to the entry facade eliminated two of three dormers, enlarged windows, and brought the roof line down to the top of the remaining dormer. A unifying trellis was carried across this area. Throughout the house, windows were enlarged and skylights added. At the rear, another trellis was added to give continuity to the front and back exteriors and provide shade to the upper windows. The plan remains as it was, except that several small rooms have been merged into a modern kitchen which extends out toward the garden and pool.

1

1&2   Exterior views
  3   Sunshades
  4   Exterior
  5   Entrance

2

3

4

5

Yang House

Design/Completion 1960/1961
Old Field, New York
Chen Nin Yang
5,400 square feet (site area: 2 acres)
Stuccoed concrete block with wood beams, wood windows, built-up roof,
sheetrock interior partitions, hardwood and carpeted floor

In this project the clients requested
a masonry house. To keep within the
budget, stuccoed concrete block was used.
The building is dug into the hillside and
the concrete block piers are perpendicular
to the view, permitting maximum areas of
glass facing Long Island Sound.

Due to the nature of block construction,
window areas to the front and sides are
minimal, resulting in good thermal
insulation. Glass areas facing the water
are protected by deep recesses and
sun shields above the view line.

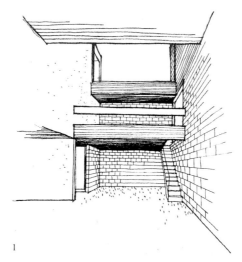

1

2

3

1   Sketch of interior
2   Front entrance
3   Rear overlooking Long Island Sound
4   Garage entry
5   Balcony
6   Entrance
7   Side deck

4

5

6

7

McCombe House

Design/Completion 1973/1974
Riverhead, New York
Leonard and Gertrude McCombe
6,500 square feet (site area: 100 acres)
Concrete footings, wood frame, stone bearing walls, horizontal cedar boards treated with preservative, local stone, plaster walls, stone and wood flooring

The site is at the top of a steep hill overlooking Long Island Sound. The building serves as a farmhouse for a 100-acre orchard. A mile-long driveway leads through magnificent groves of fruit trees and terminates in a cul-de-sac around a greenhouse. The greenhouse is the principal focus of the entrance facade and is seen against a background of stone walls that form the front of the house. A covered roof connecting the greenhouse and main structure forms a porte-cochere for vehicular access.

The main entry opens to a large hall which is the unifying vertical space that ties together the entire structure. From this space radiate the kitchen, living room, and guest room, all on the ground floor, and the four bedrooms on the second floor, each with a handsome view.

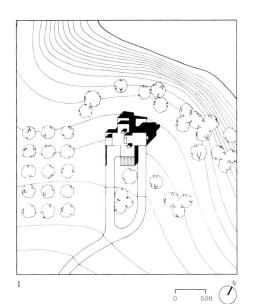

1

2

3

4

5

1   Site plan
2   Entrance hall
3   View from the north
4   View from the south
5   View from the east

Greenbriar

Design/Completion 1981/1984
Somers, New York
Greenbriar Associates
Houses ranging from 1,840 to 2,590 square feet (site area: 250 acres)
Wood frame, concrete foundations
Vertical cedar boards (exterior), painted sheetrock, hardwood and carpeted floors

The developers of this 250-acre parcel in a rural area wanted a series of house models built for sale to fit diverse living styles. The subdivision of 237 units (detached and attached) is a "planned unit development," meaning it has large areas in common and relatively small lots. To achieve a unified identity and allow for economical and efficient construction, the design uses a common modular system and stock construction elements.

The modular scheme features a horizontal and vertical module that allows house layouts to vary from unit to unit without loss of overall identity. Houses are clustered around cul-de-sacs, each having a distinctive color. Houses range from 1,840 to 2,590 square feet and feature open social areas, split levels to accommodate the hilly site, and window openings grouped toward view and sun.

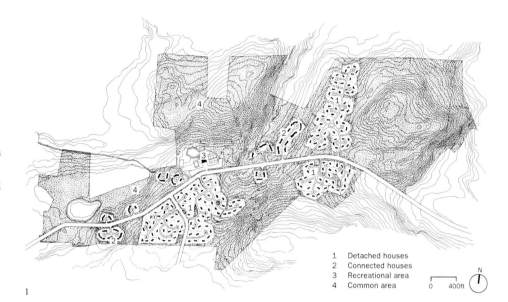

1 Detached houses
2 Connected houses
3 Recreational area
4 Common area

0   400ft   N

1

2

1   Site plan
2–7 Views of various models
8   Ground floor plan of typical model
9   Second floor plan of typical model

3   4

5

6

7

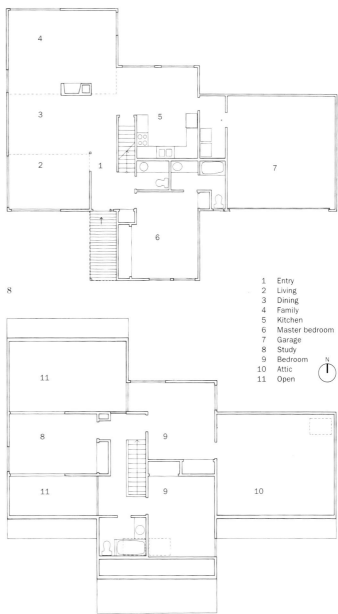

8

9

1 Entry
2 Living
3 Dining
4 Family
5 Kitchen
6 Master bedroom
7 Garage
8 Study
9 Bedroom
10 Attic
11 Open

N

Leader House

Design/Completion 1982/1983
Franklin Lakes, New Jersey
Barbara and Harold Leader
5,000 square feet (house), 700 square feet (garage) (site area: 2 acres)
Wood frame, brick solar wall, skylight with movable fabric solar shades,
sheetrock walls, hardwood and carpeted floors in bedroom area

The central feature of this open-plan house is a two-story sculptural wall designed to retain solar heat from the south-facing skylights above. Since a large amount of glass can lead to summer overheating or winter chill on sunless days, the skylights have been fitted with insulating shades keyed to automatic temperature sensors that control their movement. In addition to blocking unwanted summer sun and yielding an R-2 insulating value in the winter, they are translucent enough to provide daytime light levels that permit reading without artificial illumination. Air is vented through the skylights on warm summer days. On the lower level, a solarium, which can be closed or opened, provides a further buffer against temperature extremes.

1

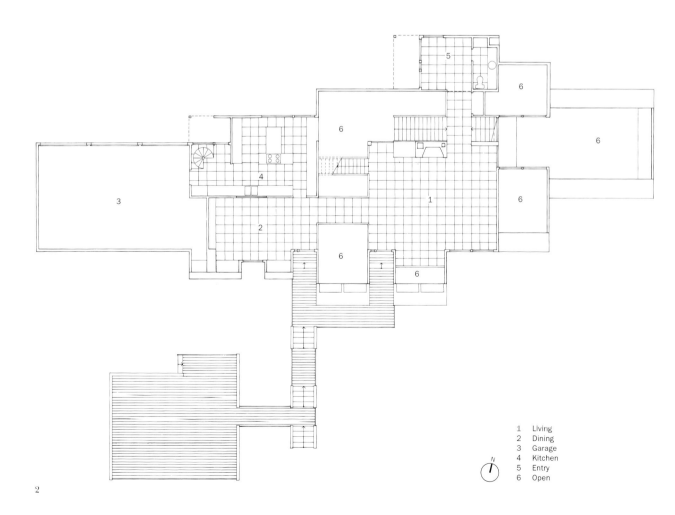

2

1 Living
2 Dining
3 Garage
4 Kitchen
5 Entry
6 Open

N

1 View showing sunshades
2 Main floor plan
3 Living room
4 Entrance side of house
5 Night view showing skylights
6&7 Living areas

3

4

5

6

7

Sara House

Design/Completion 1979/1980
Greenwich, Connecticut
Ed and Ruth Sara
3,200 square feet (site area: 4 acres)
Wood frame, concrete retaining walls and pool structure
Cedar boards stained black; sheetrock interior; stucco walls around pool;
tile, wood, and carpet floors

The clients wanted to incorporate solar gain into their house, and called on the architects after seeing a passive solar design of ours that had been published. The resulting design includes three bedrooms, an open living space, and a kitchen, and incorporates an enclosed swimming pool that serves as a heat sink for the house.

The clients requested that the house shape and the spaces within be traditional. The site posed a special problem since the pool room, with its glass roof, required a southern exposure for passive solar gain, but the site presented a lovely view to the west over a pond. The problem was to orient as many rooms as possible toward the view, while also relating them to the pool room, which is an important space in the house. Glass walls provide views into the pool room while isolating the humidity within it.

The plan is an open scheme on the main level, featuring the kitchen and a three-sided fireplace designed to be viewed from the study, living room, kitchen, and entry. The fireplace is surrounded by a sunken seating area which overlooks the pool; slanted windows enable the seated person to look down into the lower level. Interiors feature architectural elements and built-in furniture. Color is applied sparingly, with the exception of the kitchen, which is bright red.

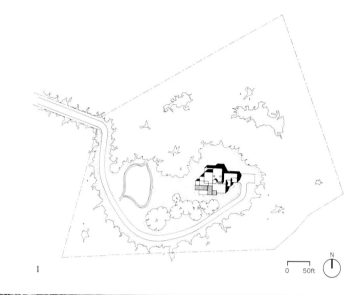

1

2

3

1 Site plan
2 Dusk view of pool room
3 View across pond
4 Section
5 Entrance
6 Pool room
7 Interior of pool room
8 Built-in furniture in bedroom

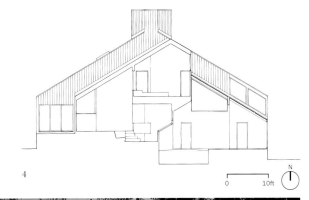

4

0   10ft

N

5

6

7

8

9   First floor plan
10 Second floor plan
11 Sunken seating area
12 Breakfast alcove and dining area

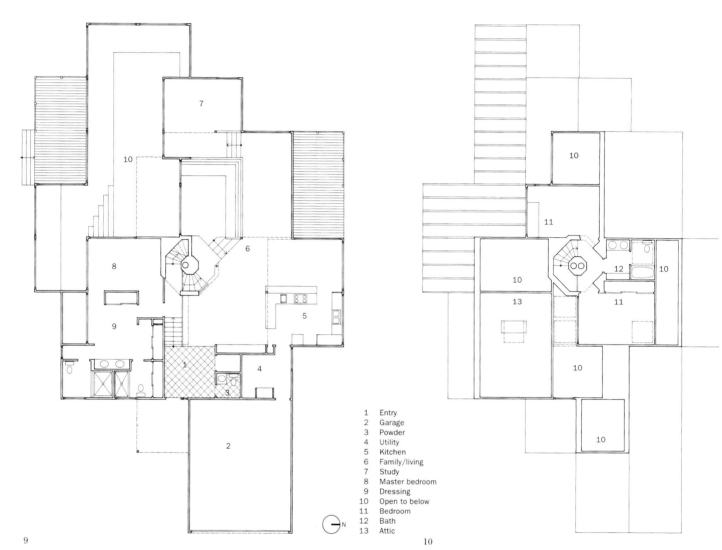

1   Entry
2   Garage
3   Powder
4   Utility
5   Kitchen
6   Family/living
7   Study
8   Master bedroom
9   Dressing
10 Open to below
11 Bedroom
12 Bath
13 Attic

9   10

11

12

Kleinman House

Design/Completion 1977/1978
Napeague, New York
The Kleinman Family
1,700 square feet (site area: 1 acre)
Wood frame on concrete footings, aluminum thermal windows, metal handrails, tile and wood floors

Situated on a sandy strip of land between a marsh and Napeague Bay, the house orients itself to the bay, which is the main view. The plan is rectangular, with secondary bedrooms on the lower level and main living areas on the second level to take advantage of the view. The plan features a series of shed-like "clip-ons," which house services such as kitchen, laundry, fireplace, and stair towers.

The seasonal aspect of the house did not mandate passive solar gain, rather the reverse. Natural cooling was achieved via through ventilation. Therefore, the south facade is mainly closed, with the exception of high windows which serve to cool the house syphonically. A cast-iron stove housed in a colorful niche is sufficient to heat the entire open area on the second floor.

1   Upper level plan
2   Site plan
3   Land side of house
4   Bay side of house
5   East elevation
6   Interior

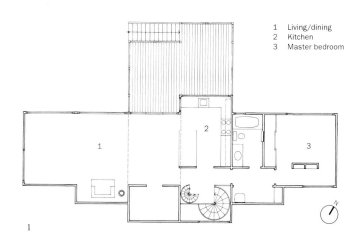

1   Living/dining
2   Kitchen
3   Master bedroom

1

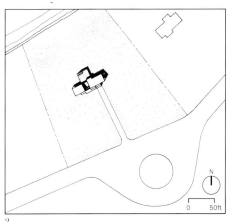

2

3

4

5

6

New Preston House

Design/Completion 1988/1989
New Preston, Connecticut
3,082 square feet (house), 800 square feet (garage) (site area: 10 acres)
Wood frame
Wood shingle cladding trimmed with painted wood, wood windows,
sheetrock interior trimmed with wood, hardwood and carpeted floors

In this Connecticut house, the architects
grouped interior spaces under a salt-box
roof flanked on the entrance side by
garage and guest house wings. The
entrance is a connected structure, built
on the axis of the house between the two
wings. Interior walls are skewed, providing
a series of vistas through the major rooms.
The walls are trimmed with bands and
pilasters of bleached pine. A two-sided
chimney is welcoming at the entrance and
can also be enjoyed from the living room.

1

2

3

4

1 Pond side of house
2&3 Exterior views
4 Entry
5 Exterior
6&7 Living area
8 Second floor plan
9 First floor plan

5

6

7

156

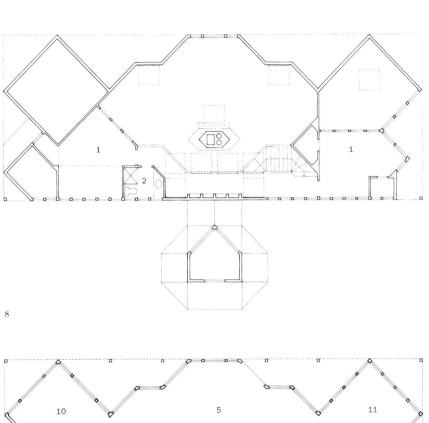

8

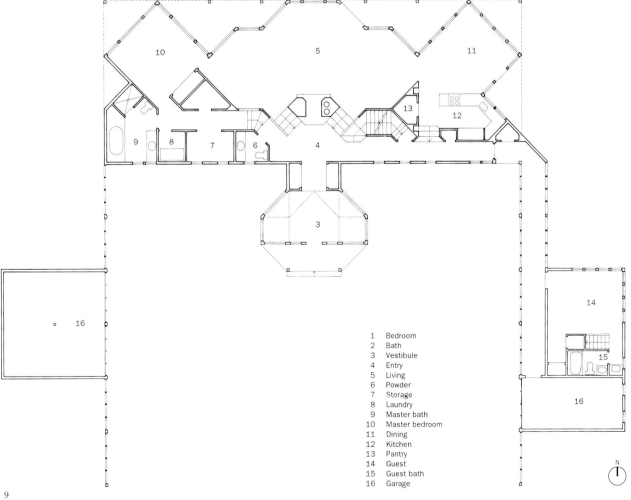

9

1   Bedroom
2   Bath
3   Vestibule
4   Entry
5   Living
6   Powder
7   Storage
8   Laundry
9   Master bath
10 Master bedroom
11 Dining
12 Kitchen
13 Pantry
14 Guest
15 Guest bath
16 Garage

Ferguson House

Design/Completion 1982/1983
Pound Ridge, New York
2,950 square feet (house), 500 square feet (garage) (site area: 2 acres)
Wood frame, concrete foundations
Ceramic tile floors, sheetrock interior, cedar ceiling

A narrow sunspace gathers and stores the sun's energy and provides a view of a nearby lake. The sunspace is separated from the living spaces by a stuccoed concrete block wall through which operable windows permit the flow of heated air on sunny winter days. The occupants are also able to operate the skylights in this sunspace for natural ventilation during the hot summer months.

1&2   Exterior views
3&4   Interior views
  5   First floor plan

1

2

3

4

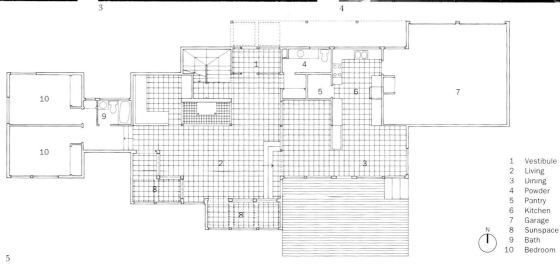

5

1   Vestibule
2   Living
3   Dining
4   Powder
5   Pantry
6   Kitchen
7   Garage
8   Sunspace
9   Bath
10 Bedroom

N

Boyle House

Design/Completion 1981/1982
Bernardsville, New Jersey
Hugh Boyle
2,210 square feet (site area: 1 acre)
Wood frame
Cedar boards (exterior), asphalt shingle roof, sheetrock (interior), slate
and wood floors

Commissioned by a couple, one of whom was handicapped, this solar house was planned in accordance with Veterans Administration standards. The design complies with regulations governing door, fixture, and corridor clearances; lever handles on doors; grab bars in bathrooms; and access ramps from the exterior. Adequate turning radii for a wheelchair was allowed for in all major rooms.

Site planning was difficult because the topography and zoning setback requirements made the best orientation (due south) impossible. As a result, the house was turned 20 degrees west of south. This entailed some loss of efficiency but still gave excellent use of passive solar energy. The plan faces all rooms and most glass areas to the south. An important feature is the sunspace which serves as an additional eating area and green zone. This space can be closed off when it radiates more heat than it gains, such as at night or during long, sunless periods in winter.

Exterior materials are natural cedar boards stained gray, asphalt shingles, and aluminum thermal windows. Interior materials include sheetrock and integrally colored concrete on the floors to provide thermal mass.

1

2

4

5

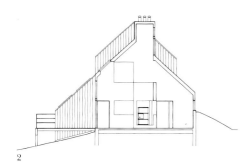

3

1   Exterior
2   Section
3   Kitchen
4   Sunspace
5   Living room

Aksen House

Design/Completion 1978/1979
Stamford, Connecticut
Mr and Mrs Howard Aksen
3,000 square feet (site area: 1 acre)
Wood frame
Vertical stained cedar boards (exterior), painted wood windows,
tile and hardwood floors

The house fronts on a pond to the south and west, with other houses and a well-trafficked street on the other sides. To concentrate on the view and give privacy within, the house is shaped around a concave curve, partially enclosing a deck. Window areas are concentrated within and adjacent to the curve. On the outer side, windows are limited in number and are located high in the rooms. Solar gain through the south windows was a consideration in the design. The roofs slope to the north, providing a series of shed-like shapes.

The living room, shaped by the exterior curved wall and sloping roof, is the most important space. The high end culminates in the fireplace and is lit from above with skylights. Windows on all three sides admit light from different angles as the sun moves across the sky. The master bedroom overlooks this major space.

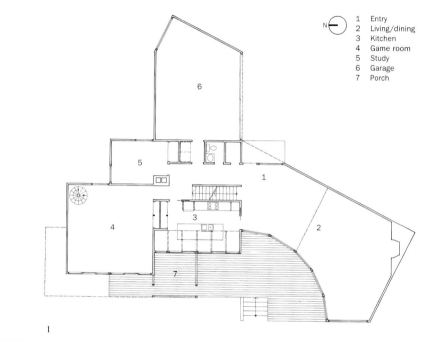

1 Entry
2 Living/dining
3 Kitchen
4 Game room
5 Study
6 Garage
7 Porch

1

1   First floor plan
2&3   Exterior views
4   Living room

2

3

4

David Alan House

Design/Completion 1991/1992
Saddle River, New Jersey
David Alan
4,300 square feet (site area: 2 acres)
Wood frame on existing foundation
Stained cedar boards, aluminum thermal windows, sheetrock, hardwood floors

The original ranch style house, was on a good residential street in a desirable neighborhood but the owner was not happy with its appearance. The architects were commissioned to upgrade the house, in particular to improve the exterior and the entrance, to bring more light into the interior, and to achieve a better flow of space.

A wide, curved staircase rises from the new entry to the main level of the house; the stair is tucked below two gables added to the original house to provide additional space and increase dimensions. Inside, the ceiling below the attic was removed to reveal interesting tie beams, which were wrapped with sheetrock to achieve another visual layer in the room. This process also opened up the spaces to give a lofty feel.

1

1 View from street
2 Living room
3 Entrance stair

2   3

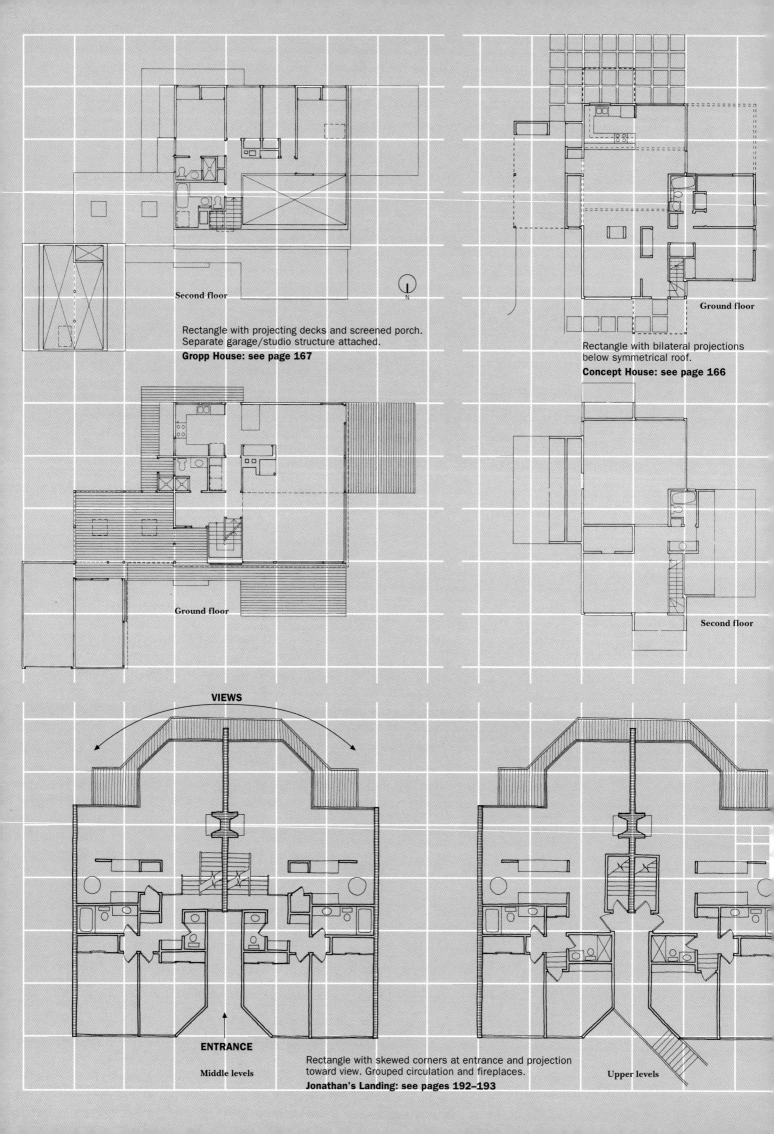

Second floor

Rectangle with projecting decks and screened porch.
Separate garage/studio structure attached.
Gropp House: see page 167

Ground floor

Rectangle with bilateral projections
below symmetrical roof.
Concept House: see page 166

Ground floor

Second floor

VIEWS

ENTRANCE

Middle levels

Rectangle with skewed corners at entrance and projection
toward view. Grouped circulation and fireplaces.
Jonathan's Landing: see pages 192–193

Upper levels

Shelter

Plan modules are useful where economy or flexibility is a goal. The plans shown on this page were intended to be used as repetitive types that could be modified for size and site variation. All plans on these pages and the following project pages are at the same scale. Refer to the module key on this page.

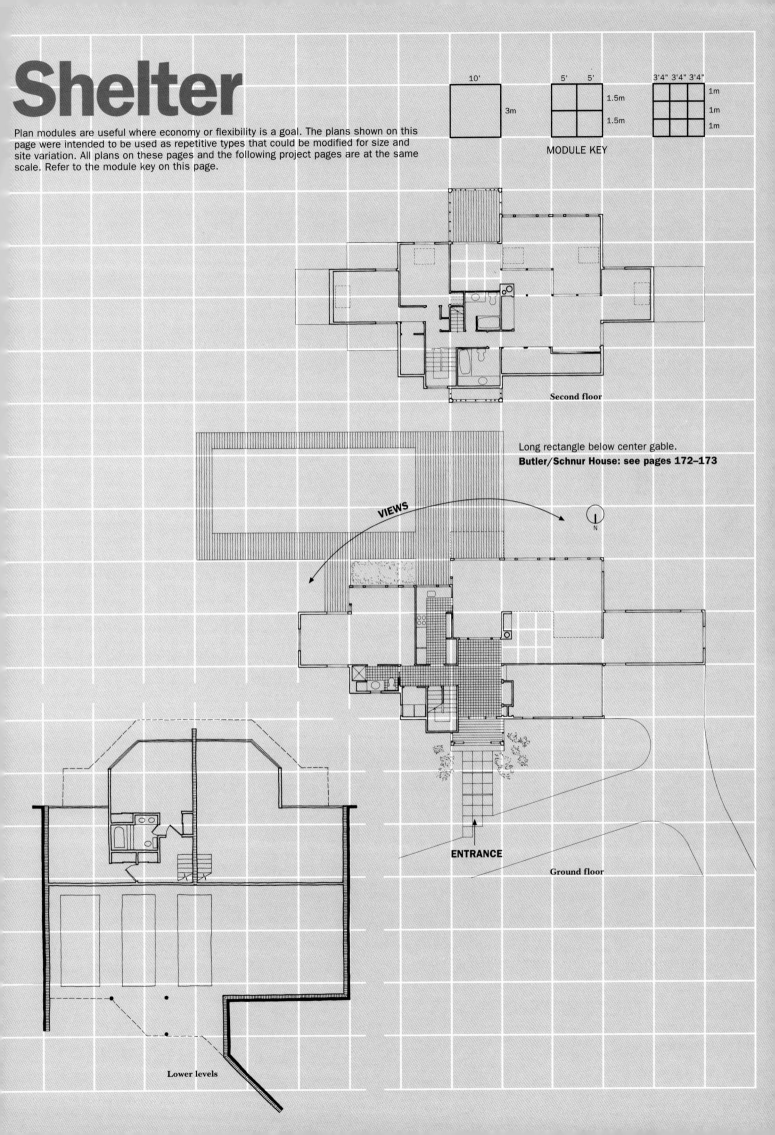

MODULE KEY

Second floor

Long rectangle below center gable.
Butler/Schnur House: see pages 172–173

VIEWS

N

ENTRANCE

Ground floor

Lower levels

Vuolo House

Design/Completion 1980/1981
Long Island, New York
Don and Ellen Vuolo
3,125 square feet (site area: 1 acre)
Wood frame
Vertical cedar siding, glass skylights with movable shutters, painted
sheetrock interiors, wood and carpet floors

With decks projecting from a closely organized central plan, this house provides a striking accent among the surrounding trees. Rooms revolve around a central stair core, providing a series of levels on which various living areas open out to the views and sunshine. The focus of the house is the master bedroom/living area which extends through two stories and is capped by skylights. These skylights are provided with movable insulation on the outside which serves to block the hot summer sun and conserve precious solar gain on winter nights.

Decks are located at the dining and living areas as well as on a high roof from which a panoramic view can be enjoyed.

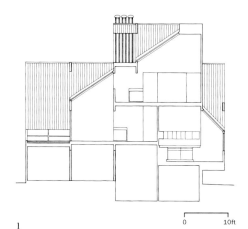

1

0   10ft

2

3

1   Section
2   Exterior
3   Axonometric
4   Exterior with solar shades drawn
5   Living room
6   Interior with solar shades drawn
7   Interior with solar shades raised
8   Upper level plan
9   Lower level plan
10 Middle level plan

4

164

5

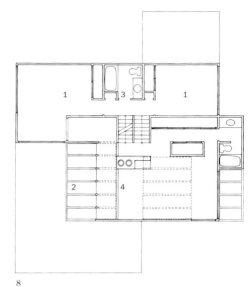

8

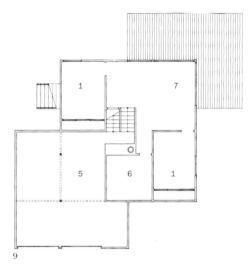

9

10

6

7

1   Bedroom
2   Open to below
3   Bath
4   Master bedroom
5   Garage
6   Mechanical
7   Recreational
8   Powder
9   Entry
10 Living
11 Dining
12 Kitchen

Concept House

Design/Completion 1978/1979
Lancaster, Pennsylvania
Better Homes and Gardens/Armstrong
1,300 square feet (site area: 0.3 acre)
Wood frame on concrete slab, prefinished plywood exterior, asphalt shingle roof, wood windows, painted sheetrock interiors, tile and wood floors

This house was commissioned by *Better Homes and Gardens* magazine to explore the idea of good, workable, affordable housing. Three architects from three different geographical areas were invited to come up with plans for a small, economical house that would meet the needs of a typical family.

The plan shows how a family could start in a small way, with a single level. As the family and budget grew, the upstairs could be finished, a bedroom added, and the garage enclosed.

At the heart of the house is the high-ceilinged family room, open to its surroundings to increase its apparent size. The spacious master suite, designed to accommodate a home office or study, overlooks the family room. The living room is small and is centered on a two-sided fireplace.

The simple, direct styling of this house is designed to fit into any neighborhood. Demonstration models have been well received in many cities.

1   Plan
2   Sketch
3   Interior
4&5   Exterior views

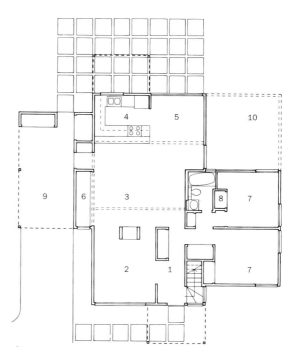

1   Entry/stair
2   Living
3   Family
4   Kitchen
5   Garden room/dining
6   Hobby center
7   Bedroom
8   Bath
9   Carport or garage
10 Future bedroom

1

2

3

4

5

Gropp House

Design/Completion 1979/1980
Addition 1995
Quogue, New York
Lou and Jane Gropp
1,700 square feet (site area: 2 acres)
Wood frame
Vertical boards (exterior), painted sheetrock (interior), tile and wood floors

The owners and architect agreed that the house was to be simple and reflective of traditional house forms in the area. The plan separates active living areas on the lower floor from the sleeping quarters on the second floor, with a separate activities/guest building on the side.

Orientations are to the south and west for solar gain. An active domestic hot water system is installed on the south-facing roof of the outbuilding. Movable shutters are provided over large glass areas to conserve heat in the winter and keep the house cool in the summer.

1

2

3

4

1–3   Exterior views
  4   Interior
  5   Ground floor plan
  6   Interior living room

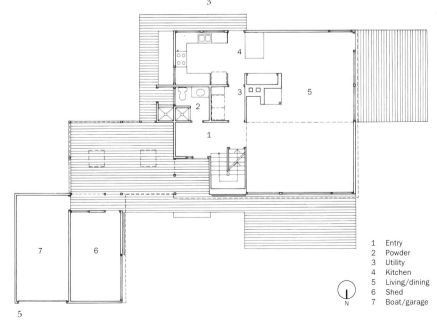

5

1   Entry
2   Powder
3   Utility
4   Kitchen
5   Living/dining
6   Shed
7   Boat/garage

N

6

Morton House

Design/Completion 1984/1985
Middletown, New Jersey
Chris and Leslie Morton
2,650 square feet (house), 420 square feet (garage) (site area: 1 acre)
Wood frame
Vertical boards (exterior), wood windows, fiberglass shingles, sheetrock
(interior), carpet and tile floors

In this project, the clients felt a traditional house form would suite their locale. Inside, however, they wanted the lively functional spaces of contemporary architecture. To achieve these goals, the architects arranged flat-roofed diagonal wings within a long gabled roof. The geometry of the wings and the straight lines of the gabled portion of the house create attractive spaces within.

The entrance side of the house offers privacy and is embellished with a trellis. The back of the house features a multi-windowed living area oriented to the fireplace and the views.

1

2

3

1 Exterior
2 Interior of living room
3 Exterior at night
4 Kitchen
5 View into living room from above
6 Living room
7 Second floor plan
8 First floor plan
9 Entrance

4

5

6

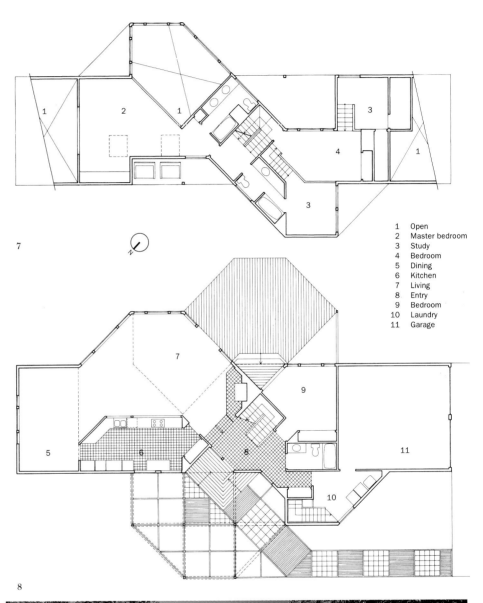

7

8

1 Open
2 Master bedroom
3 Study
4 Bedroom
5 Dining
6 Kitchen
7 Living
8 Entry
9 Bedroom
10 Laundry
11 Garage

9

Rothschild House

Design/Completion 1978/1979
Greenwich, Connecticut
Mr and Mrs Richard Rothschild
3,000 square feet (site area: 1 acre)
Wood frame
Unstained vertical cedar boards (exterior); painted sheetrock (interior);
wood windows; carpet, wood, and tile floors

The site is part of an old estate which had been split into building lots. Many fine old trees remained on the land and the house had to be carefully sited among them.

A carefully written program documented the client's need for two major living spaces—a family room/kitchen and a music room. The music room is acoustically isolated from the other spaces, while the family room looks out on the park-like setting. Internal zoning places the master bedroom and guest room on the first floor at opposite ends of the house. Children's bedrooms are on the second floor.

Sloping roofs were mandatory, and the spaces of the house are grouped beneath a series of gable roofs arranged to provide a spatial focus at the hearth, where roof windows spill light onto the vertical element of the chimneys. The house is oriented for solar gain, with the majority of the windows and roof windows facing south. Solar collectors are provided for domestic hot water.

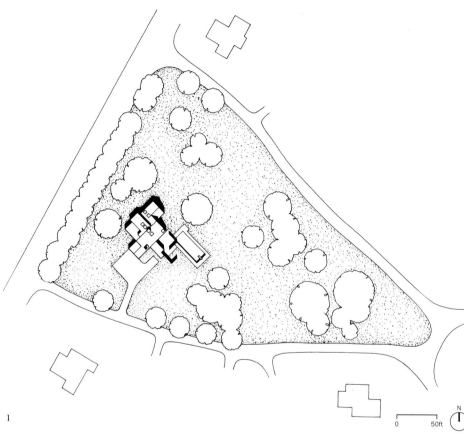

1

2

1   Site plan
2   Exterior
3   Music room
4   Living room
5   Section
6   Ground floor plan

3

4

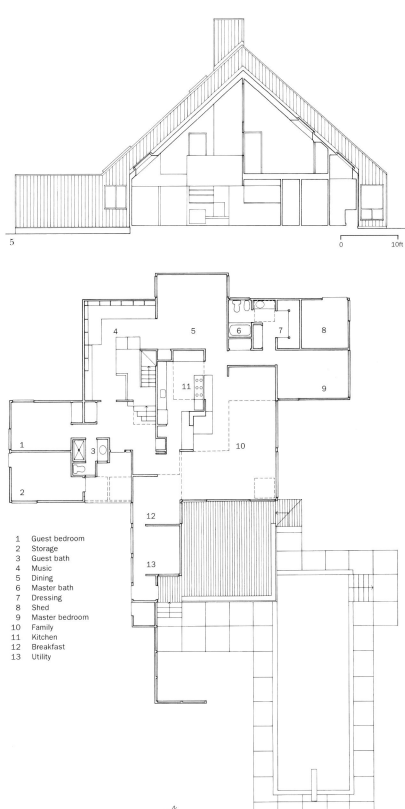

5

6

1   Guest bedroom
2   Storage
3   Guest bath
4   Music
5   Dining
6   Master bath
7   Dressing
8   Shed
9   Master bedroom
10 Family
11 Kitchen
12 Breakfast
13 Utility

Butler/Schnur House, 10 White Pine Road

Design/Completion 1984/1985
East Hampton, New York
Jerry Butler and Leslie Schnur
2,700 square feet (site area: 2 acres)
Wood frame
Horizontal cedar siding with corner boards, aluminum windows, sheetrock interior, wide board pine floors

The design of the house seeks to combine the free, projecting volumes of Modernism with the sloped roof forms and techniques of traditional architecture. Most of the living functions are grouped under a common roof, while individual rooms project beyond it to catch the views.

The projections are lean-tos, recalling the vernacular of early Colonial and shingle-style architecture. Other stylistic influences are reflected in the use of cedar siding applied horizontally rather than vertically, with corner boards, another reference to Colonial detailing.

The house is energy-efficient, with most glass facing south, and insulated walls and roofs.

1

1   Entrance
2   Rear at night
3   End view
4   Ground floor plan
5&6 Second floor interior balcony
7   Living room

2

3

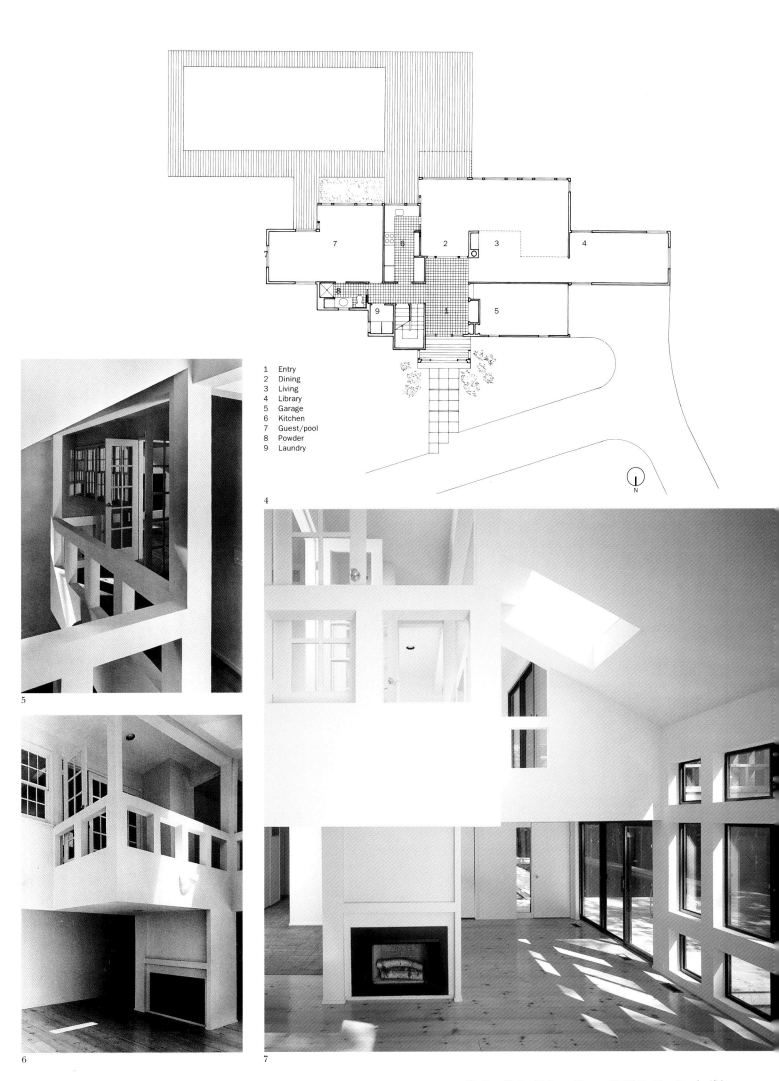

1 Entry
2 Dining
3 Living
4 Library
5 Garage
6 Kitchen
7 Guest/pool
8 Powder
9 Laundry

4

5

6

7

Frocht House

Design/Completion 1987/1988
East Hampton, New York
Dr and Mrs Alexander Frocht
3,560 square feet (site area: 2 acres)
Wood frame, vertical stained cedar boards (exterior), painted
sheetrock (interior), tile and wood floors

Designed for collectors of contemporary
and primitive art, the interior space is lofty
and colorful, enlivened by architectural
detail. Interior colors complement the
natural materials, while other hues
highlight the pilasters, trim, and grilles.
On the exterior, the vertical siding is
stained black. The entrance is emphasized
in lighter gray and a frieze-like detail strip
under the roof is also painted gray.
Furniture, custom-designed by the
architects, is of ash decorated with
inserts of various woods.

The rectangular plan has bowed walls at
the front and also at the back, where
a two-story window looks out over the
evergreen landscape.

1

1&2   Exterior front
  3   Living room
  4   Ground floor plan
  5   Second floor plan

2

174

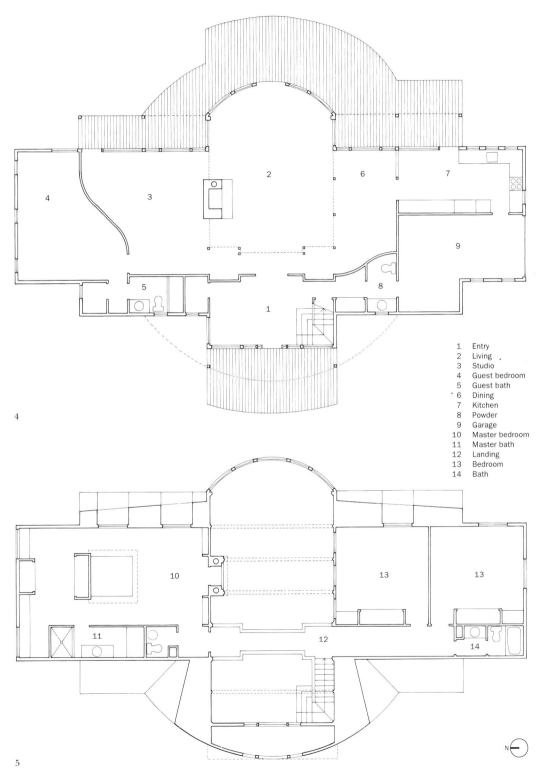

1	Entry
2	Living
3	Studio
4	Guest bedroom
5	Guest bath
6	Dining
7	Kitchen
8	Powder
9	Garage
10	Master bedroom
11	Master bath
12	Landing
13	Bedroom
14	Bath

4

3

5

N

6   Sketch of living room
7–9 Living room
10   Entrance
11   Living room at night
Opposite:
   Dining room

6

7

8

10

11

9

Kessler House

Design/Completion 1995/1996
Charlotte, North Carolina
Fred and Jane Kessler
1,800 square feet (site area: 3 acres)
Wood frame, concrete retaining walls, insulation finish (exterior), wood windows, sheetrock and tile (interior)

Built into a south-facing hillside, this house captures the view and incorporates energy-saving features to utilize solar gain. The owners, who are craftspeople, designed some of the features, such as an ornamental steel trellis, a range hood, and custom tiles for the fireplace and counter tops.

The two-bedroom plan focuses on the central kitchen/living/dining area, where spaces are generous and the ceiling is high.

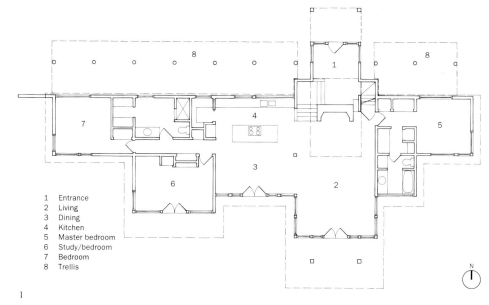

1 Entrance
2 Living
3 Dining
4 Kitchen
5 Master bedroom
6 Study/bedroom
7 Bedroom
8 Trellis

1

2

3

1 Plan
2 Entrance
3 Front showing trellis
4 Rear view
5 Entrance
6 Detail of exterior
7 Kitchen
8 Fireplace
9 Interior

4

5

6

7

8

9

Wright House

Design/Completion 1987/1988
Guilford, Connecticut
Dr and Mrs Kim Wright
2,960 square feet (site area: 3 acres)
Wood frame
Stained vertical cedar boards, square fixed and sliding windows, painted
sheetrock interior

The design emphasizes various geometric elements, both in its architectural form and in the use of color. For example, the roof and gable end is separated from the walls below by a band of recessed windows, stained in a contrasting color. The same principle is used to visually separate the chimney mass from the house, and also in the curved forms which protrude from the simple rectangular form of the house.

The concept is continued on the interior. Here, the color is applied in layers. In one instance, a gray layered grid on a yellow background overlays the window pattern. The wall is capped by another color band encasing the high windows.

The family room furniture and the banquette in the living room were designed by the architects. The forms are upholstered and soft, in contrast to the geometry of the walls.

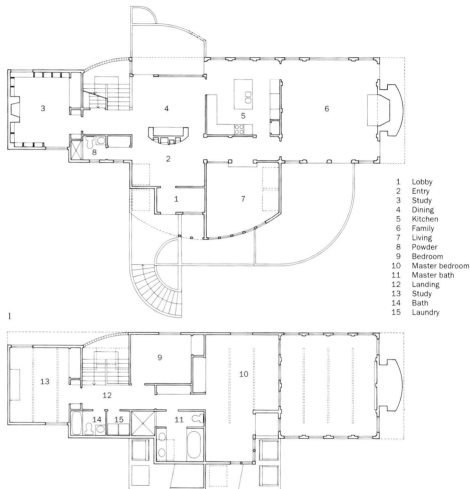

1 Lobby
2 Entry
3 Study
4 Dining
5 Kitchen
6 Family
7 Living
8 Powder
9 Bedroom
10 Master bedroom
11 Master bath
12 Landing
13 Study
14 Bath
15 Laundry

1

3

2

4

5

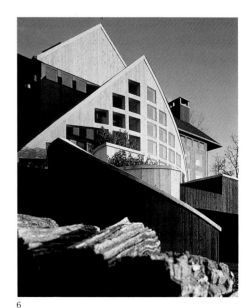

6

1 First floor plan
2 Exterior
3 Second floor plan
4–6 Exterior views
7 Working drawing
8 Living room
9 Stair
10 Interior detail

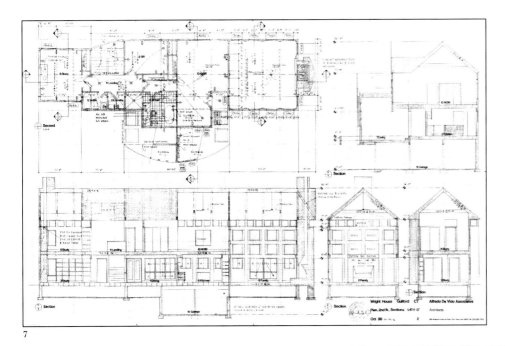

7

8

9

10

The Royale

Design/Completion 1986/1987
New York, New York
Eichner Properties Inc.
Design Architect: Alfredo De Vido
Project Architect: Schuman Lichtenstein Claman & Efron
Lobby Architect: Voorsanger & Mills Associates
Landscape Architect: Quennell/Rothschild Associates
241,000 square feet (site area: 20,083 square feet)
Concrete, flat slab construction
Brick finish (exterior), exposed concrete slab edges, insulated sheetrock
on metal studs (interior), aluminum thermal windows

Real estate professionals recognize the desirability of large apartments on high floors with good views. To meet this demand, the architects designed a building on Manhattan's East Side that places larger apartments and duplexes on upper floors, and studio and one-bedroom units on lower floors. To achieve the required area, the floors are cantilevered at the 26th floor and again at the 35th floor.

The facade of the tower consists of brick piers combined with a glass curtain wall. The cruciform shape provides all major rooms with views in two directions. The beveled corners accentuate the view from within the apartments.

The building is topped by a four-sided pyramid and lantern which conceal the elevator machine rooms and water tower. The lantern will illuminate the top of the building at night.

Retail and commercial space is provided on the Third Avenue frontage and on a portion of the 64th Street frontage, where a plaza provides access to the condominium tower. A public plaza on 63rd Street to the south features planting areas and seating, and provides access to retail areas.

1

2

3

4

1&2   Exterior views
3&4   Exterior details
  5   Entrance court

5

6 Plan of penthouse floor
7 Plan of one-bedroom and studio floor
Opposite:
   Lobby

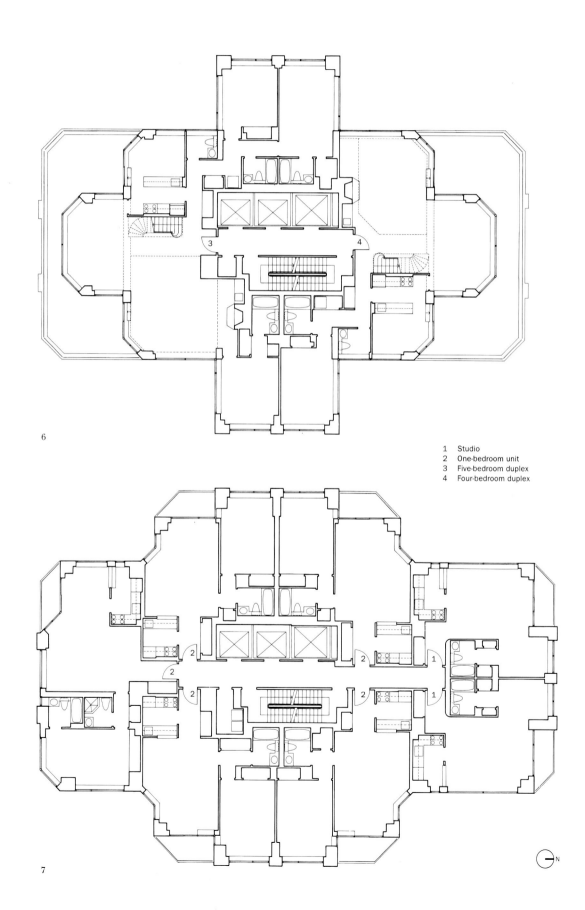

6

1 Studio
2 One-bedroom unit
3 Five-bedroom duplex
4 Four-bedroom duplex

7

222 Columbia Heights

Design/Completion 1979/1980
Brooklyn, New York
Bruce Eichner
3,800 square feet (triplex); 570 square feet (rental);
1,320 and 670 square feet (condominiums)
Masonry exterior wall, brick cladding, interior sheetrock, steel "C" joists
for floor constuction, hardwood floor, tinted precast concrete

Brooklyn Heights, a Landmarks Preservation District within New York City, is noted for its four-story brownstone houses, many of which were completed in the late 19th century in the Renaissance Revival style.

Blending a contemporary house with older neighbors at first posed a problem. The client's original program would have led to a two- to three-story house being built on a vacant piece of land at the end of a row of handsome brownstones. However, talks with the Landmarks Preservation Commission led to a revision in this program, the effect of which was to make the height of the building equal to that of the adjacent structures. (The house now contains a triplex unit, two condominium units, and a rental unit.)

The architects' design respects the character of the original buildings. These houses are made up of a closed masonry wall, punctured regularly with windows which are large at the parlor floor and become smaller in the upper stories. They often come with an unusual entrance feature, a bay window, and a picturesque skyline.

Continued

1

2

1 Sketch
2 Exterior
Opposite:
    Living room with view of Manhattan

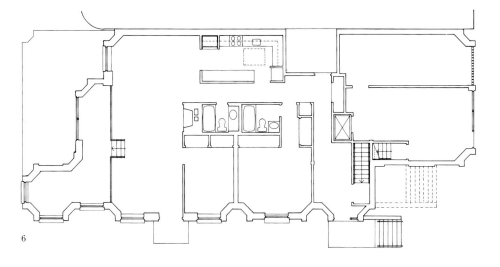

6

The new building provides the same
arrangement of openings, enlivened by
cornices and belt courses. Within, spaces
are contemporary in shape, thereby
increasing the apparent size of the rooms.
Generous window areas bring natural light
to all parts of the house while offering a
splendid view of lower Manhattan.

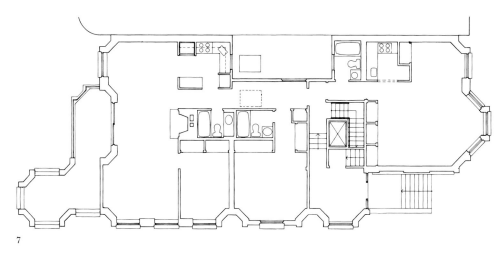

7

4

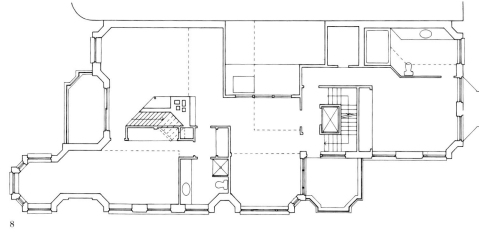

8

5

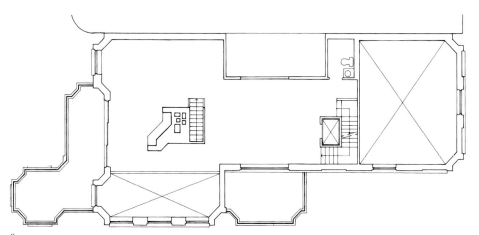

9

10

4   Entrance
5   Kitchen
6   Lower level condominium plan
7   Parlor/condominium/rental plan
8   Triplex first floor plan
9   Triplex roof level plan
10   Detail
11   View toward Manhattan
12   Dining area
13   Harbor view
14   Dining area

12

11

13

14

54 Willow Street

Design/Completion 1986/1987
Brooklyn, New York
Jonathan Eichner
11,260 square feet
Brick veneer on steel frame, lightweight steel floor joists topped with concrete
Sheetrock interior finish, hardwood floors, tile entries and wet rooms

The developer proposed a new eight-unit building for a district protected by New York City's landmark laws. The architects' solution was acceptable to both the Landmarks Preservation Commission and the local community. The scale of the new building is in keeping with the location, and its height ties in with that of the adjacent corner building. The detailing, which includes a cornice at the top of the building, an entrance feature, compatible brick color and jointing pattern, and a rusticated base, also respects the existing block, as does the arrangement of the windows.

The entrance, located in the middle for reasons of planning and efficient apartment layout, is the facade's main embellishment, featuring a two-story columned recess. The eight apartments are simplexes and duplexes of two or three bedrooms, all with views to the rear garden and the street.

1

2

3

1   Street view
2   Entrance
3   Street facade
4&5 Upper duplex plans
6   Second and third floor plan
7   Ground level plan
8   First floor plan

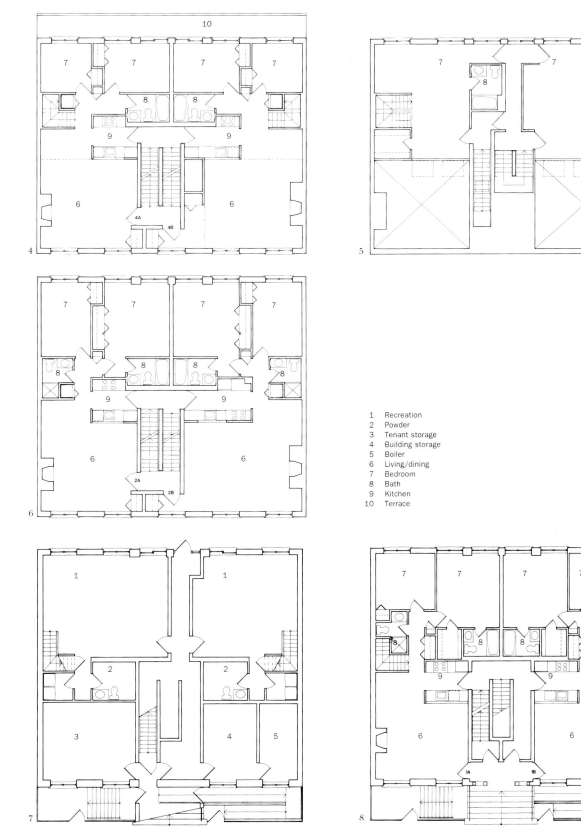

1   Recreation
2   Powder
3   Tenant storage
4   Building storage
5   Boiler
6   Living/dining
7   Bedroom
8   Bath
9   Kitchen
10   Terrace

Jonathan's Landing

Design 1985
Brooklyn, New York
Jonathan Eichner
24 units in 12 buildings
90,000 square feet (site area: 1 acre)
Wood frame, brick veneer, concrete block party walls
Sheetrock interior, hardwood and carpet floors

This 24-unit project was designed for a site on the largely abandoned Brooklyn waterfront. All 24 units face the water and are arranged in a split-level scheme; entry to the three and a half story structure is at the mid-level of the building. From this point, the occupants go either up or down to their units.

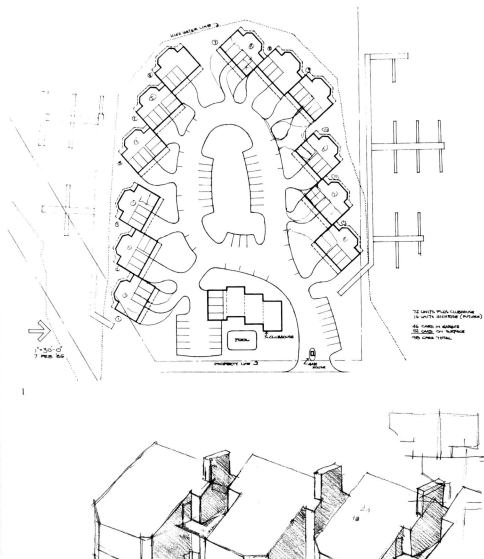

1

2

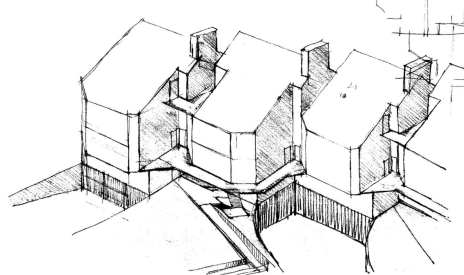

3

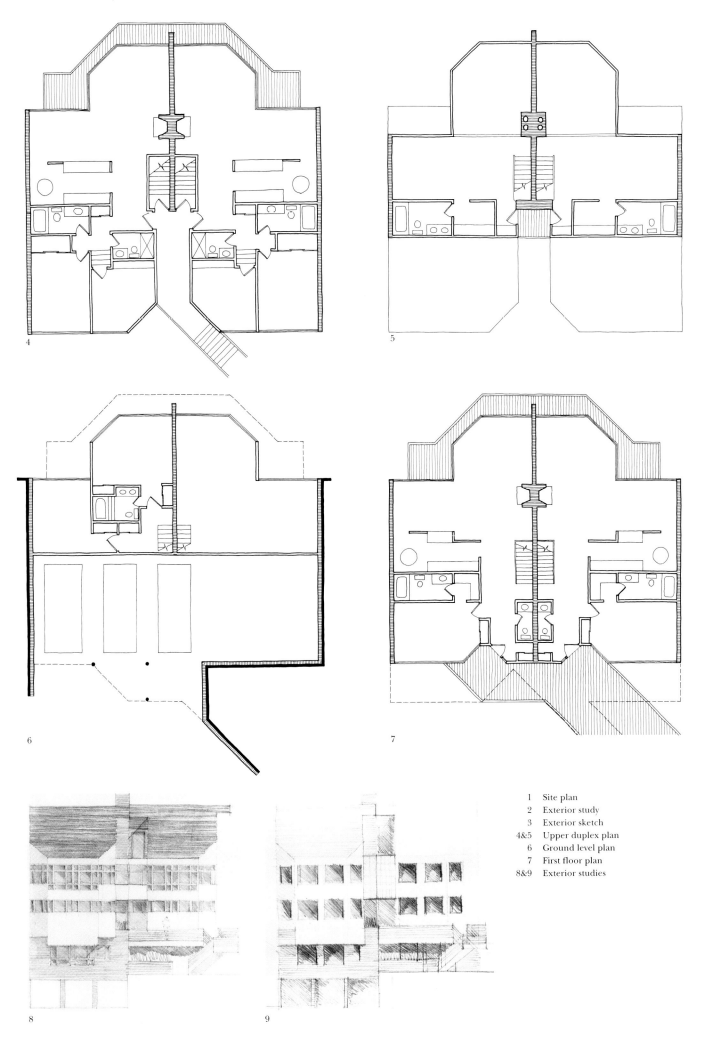

1   Site plan
2   Exterior study
3   Exterior sketch
4&5   Upper duplex plan
6   Ground level plan
7   First floor plan
8&9   Exterior studies

Apartment, 61 East 86 Street

Design/Completion 1988/1989
New York, New York
Alfredo and Catherine De Vido
Interior Designer: Catherine De Vido
Existing structure
Sheetrock, wood built-in cabinets, wood trim, wood and tile floors

In the course of renovating this 1898 apartment, detail was brought back to the rooms by adding a trilinear series of moldings that unified disparate heights of windows and doors. These painted moldings provided a transition in the progression of color from walls to ceilings.

As part of the renovation, the entry was enlarged; rooms were reconfigured; new floors were added, inset with marble areas; the kitchen and baths were replaced; and a new ceiling with built-in lighting was installed. Throughout the apartment, storage units and closets were provided for books, music, clothing, and a collection of ceramics and oriental art.

The dining room/library was paneled in wood stained light gray. Free-standing heating pipes and radiators were built in, as were below-window air conditioners. Custom window treatments were applied and new furniture was custom-designed to complement the owners' antique pieces.

1

2

1 Living
2 Dining
3 Vestible
4 Bathroom
5 Kitchen
6 Master bathroom
7 Master bedroom
8 Gallery
9 Guest room

N

1 Dining room
2 Living room
3 Plan
4 Hall

5

6

7

8

5   Living room looking towards dining room
6   Living room
7&8   Bedrooms
9   Dining room
10   Hall
11   Kitchen
12   Bath

9

10

11

12

Cohalan House

Design/Completion 1983/1984
Bayport, New York
Mary Lou Cohalan
2,350 square feet (site area: 1 acre)
Wood frame
Natural cedar boards (exterior), painted sheetrock (interior),
natural oak floors

To gain a view of a nearby inlet and to avoid problems with a high water table, the two main living floors of this house were raised above a partially bermed lower level. On the upper levels, projections and recesses in the square plan allow balconies and skylights to capture views or bring light down to key areas such as the kitchen and entry. A skylight delivers plenty of light to what would otherwise be a dark lowest level. With the architect's help, the owner served as contractor, reducing costs by approximately 20 percent.

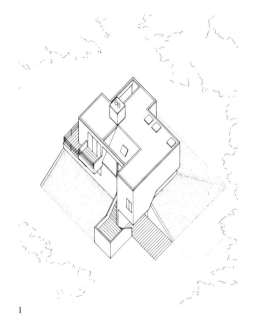

1

2

3

1 Axonometric
2 View from second level
3 Exterior
4 Stair view
5 Living room
6 Upper level plan
7 Middle level plan
8 Ground level plan

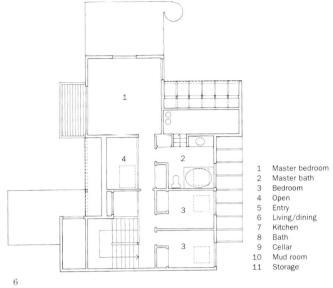

6

1 Master bedroom
2 Master bath
3 Bedroom
4 Open
5 Entry
6 Living/dining
7 Kitchen
8 Bath
9 Cellar
10 Mud room
11 Storage

4

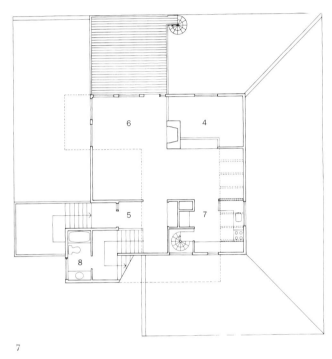

7

5

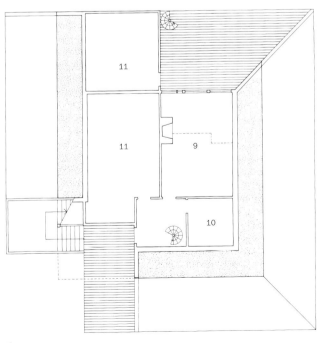

8

Staten Island House

Design/Completion 1986/1988
Staten Island, New York
6,500 square feet (site area: 0.25 acre)
Wood frame
Wood windows, brick veneer with colored mortar, struck joints,
sheetrock interior, slate roofs

The site was a small lot in a borough of
New York City. The setbacks from adjacent
houses were small and the design evolved
as an inward-looking structure with rooms
grouped around a central toplit space.

The second floor bedroom is provided
with high pyramidal ceilings and clerestory
windows to admit light to the space below.
Two stairs to the upper floor ensure
privacy to the bedrooms in each wing.

1

2

3

4

5

1	Rendering
2–5	Exterior views
6	Ground floor plan
7	Second floor plan
8	Exterior detail
9&10	Interior views

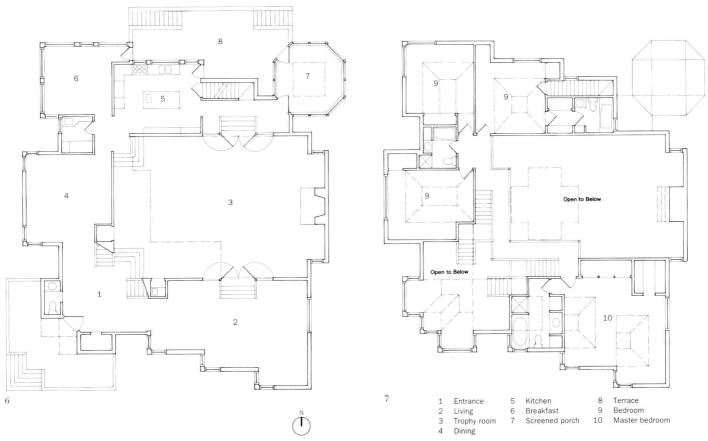

6

7

1	Entrance	5	Kitchen	8	Terrace	
2	Living	6	Breakfast	9	Bedroom	
3	Trophy room	7	Screened porch	10	Master bedroom	
4	Dining					

8

9

10

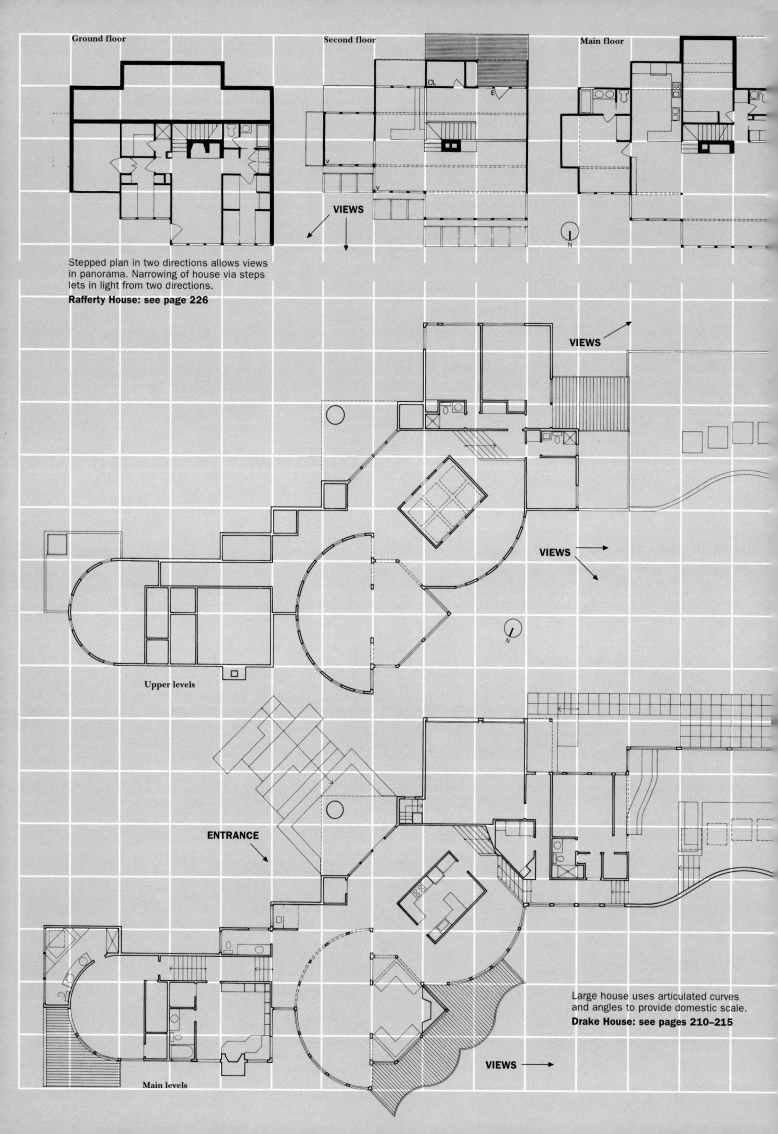

Ground floor

Second floor

Main floor

VIEWS

Stepped plan in two directions allows views
in panorama. Narrowing of house via steps
lets in light from two directions.
Rafferty House: see page 226

VIEWS

VIEWS

N

Upper levels

ENTRANCE

Large house uses articulated curves
and angles to provide domestic scale.
Drake House: see pages 210–215

VIEWS

Main levels

CL

E

V

V

N

Shelter

Curves and angles are a good plan device to orient the house toward a view or direct a series of spaces. An angled or curved wall can enliven interior spaces. All plans on these pages and the following project pages are at the same scale. Refer to the module key on this page.

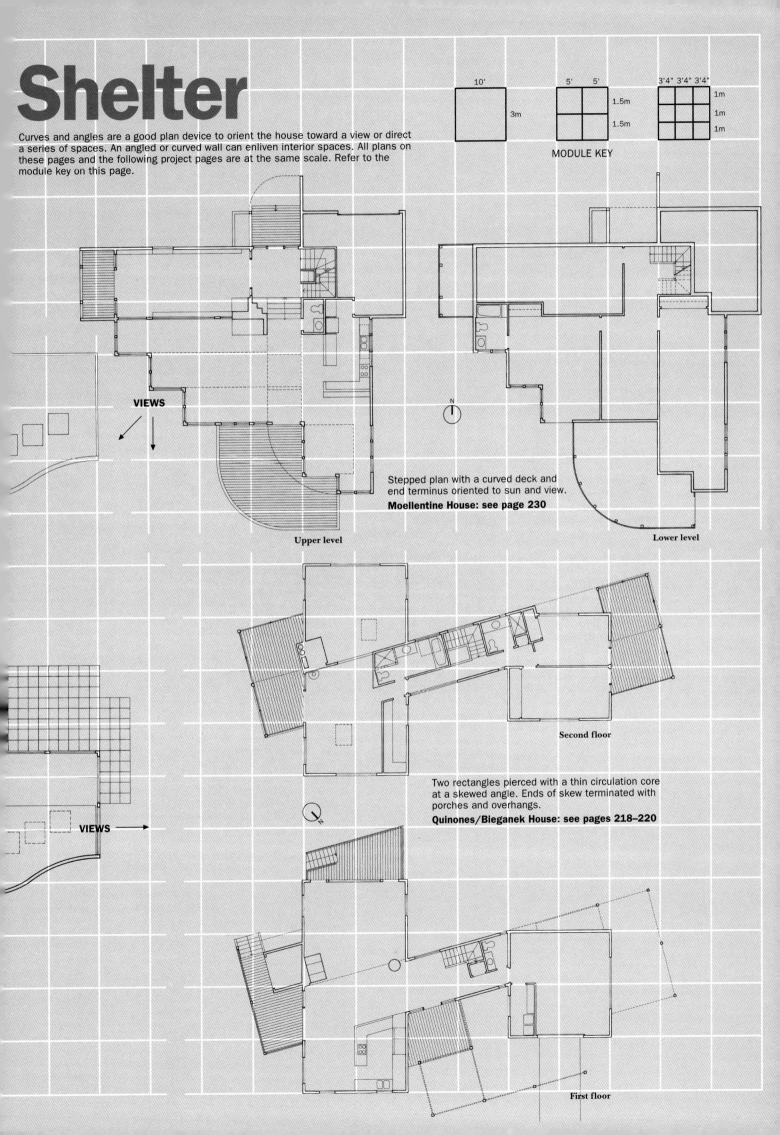

MODULE KEY

10'

3m

5' 5'

1.5m

1.5m

3'4" 3'4" 3'4"

1m

1m

1m

VIEWS

Stepped plan with a curved deck and end terminus oriented to sun and view.
Moellentine House: see page 230

Upper level

N

Lower level

Second floor

Two rectangles pierced with a thin circulation core at a skewed angle. Ends of skew terminated with porches and overhangs.
Quinones/Bieganek House: see pages 218–220

VIEWS

N

First floor

McConomy Poolhouse, Garden, and Pavilions

Design/Completion 1990/1997
Pittsburgh, Pennsylvania
Thomas and Eileen McConomy
3,100 square feet (poolhouse);
7,500 square feet (four separate garden structures)
Poolhouse: brick and brick veneer over wood frame, exterior insulating
finishing system on walls and ceiling, tile accent pattern, clad wood
windows and skylights, concrete pool, interior impervious finish
Garden buildings: exterior wood and brick on wood frame, coated wood
windows, slate roofs, stone retaining walls, natural wood interiors with
sheetrock

When the owners of this handsome brick
house completed renovations to the
existing structure, they asked the
architects to add an enclosed swimming
pool. In the resulting design, the large
structure was harmonized with the house
by using similar brick and slate as building
materials. The shaped windows in the new
addition also recall those of the earlier
house.

Inside, the poolhouse has a character
all its own. A pattern of skylights bring
in natural light in the daytime, while night
lighting enhances the space and extends
the hours of use of the pool. Bright glass
tile patterns on the walls add sparkle and
color. Mechanical systems provide proper
humidity and temperature control within
the space, an important consideration in
an attached poolhouse.

A later project, built in 1996–97,
developed an adjacent piece of land into a
garden house for family gatherings; a pair
of connected studios that serve the owners
in their artistic pursuits; and a garden
shed building. The complex is built
around a garden developed by the
architect, at the center of which is a rill
that connects the new structures visually
and terminates in a pond below the
garden house. Landscaping is simple,
using ground covers and existing fine old
trees around the rill.

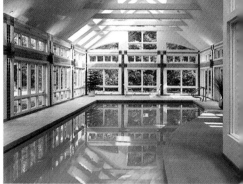

1

2

1   Exterior of poolhouse
2&3   Interior of poolhouse
4   Second floor plan
5   First floor plan
6&7   Interior views

3

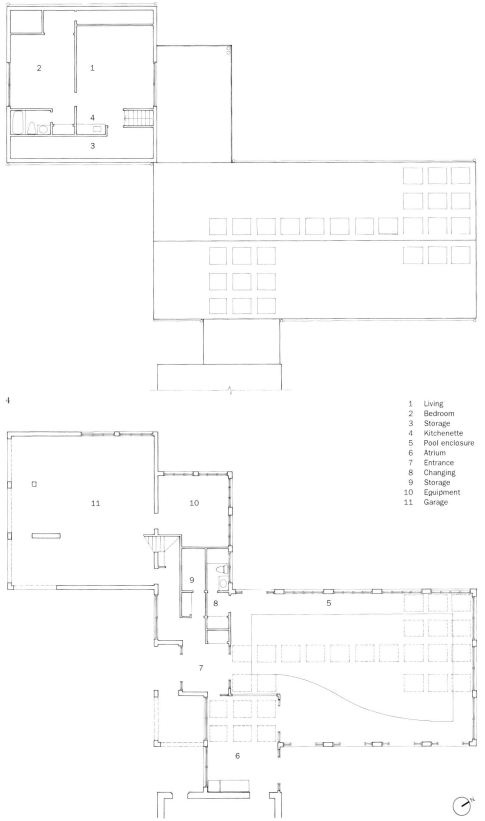

6

7

1 Living
2 Bedroom
3 Storage
4 Kitchenette
5 Pool enclosure
6 Atrium
7 Entrance
8 Changing
9 Storage
10 Equipment
11 Garage

4

5

8

9

10

11

12

13

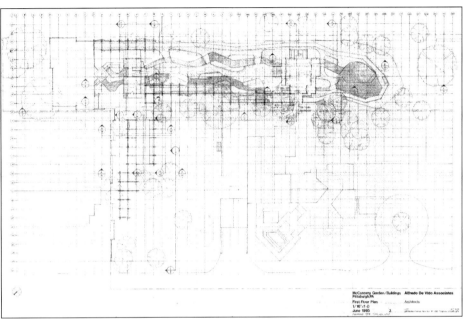

14

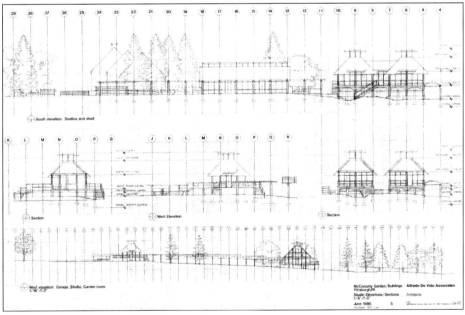

15

8   Exterior of garden house
9   Streams and sundial
10 Shed
11 Garden house
12 Studios
13 Shed and studios
14 Site plan
15 Elevations and site sections

16   Garden house
17   Studios

16

17

Trosin House

Design/Completion 1990/1991
Saltaire, Fire Island, New York
Mr and Mrs Walter Trosin
2,630 square feet (site area: 1 acre)
Wood frame
Stained wood shingles for siding and roof, hardwood floors, painted
sheetrock walls

The village of Saltaire on Fire Island has a strong architectural vernacular that works well in its exposed seaside location. Its characteristics are low, sloping roofs, deep overhangs and porches, finely scaled windows and doors, and materials that weather well in the moist climate. Houses are constructed on piers above the frequently flooded landscape.

This house adheres to the local style, fitting main living areas on the first elevated level, bedrooms on the second level, and a roof deck at the peak. Village regulations dictated the height of the house. Within, a beamed ceiling and natural wood floors frame vistas through the abundant windows.

1

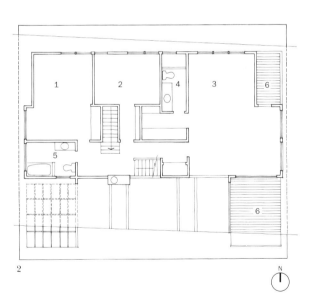

2

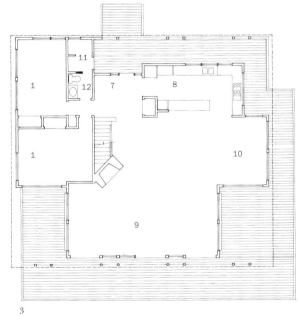

3

1   Bedroom
2   Study
3   Master bedroom
4   Master bath
5   Bath
6   Deck
7   Entry
8   Kitchen
9   Living
10 Dining
11 Shower
12 Powder

1   Exterior
2   Second floor plan
3   Ground floor plan
4   Living room
5   Exterior

4

5

Drake House

Design/Completion 1987/1988
Pound Ridge, New York
Rod and Lenir Drake
5,700 square feet (site area: 5 acres)
Wood frame
Vertical stained cedar boards (exterior cladding), painted sheetrock
(interior), hardwood floors, stucco and Brazilian hardwood
(interior pool enclosure)

Sloping gently toward the lake, this rural site is bounded by a cliff on one side and protected wetlands on the other. These factors limited the buildable area of the 5-acre property. Other important considerations in planning the house included the request for an indoor swimming pool, and the desirability that as many rooms as possible face the lake.

Our solution was to place the entry to the house at mid-level on the hill, with other rooms stepping up and down from it via internal stairs. The rooms are fitted into the hillside.

In the central part of the house, space flows freely from area to area. Various spaces are lent visual drama by their individual shapes, separate walls, and colonnades. Rooms are planned so that light enters from a variety of directions and windows capture the view.

On the lowest level is the swimming pool area, where a curving wall undulates toward the lake, fancifully adding a symbolic wave form to the water.

1

2

3

1&2   Model
3–5   Exterior views

4

5

6   Entrance (interior)
7   First floor plan
8   Exterior view
9   Dining room
10 Sketch of dining room
11 Sketch of entrance (interior)
12 Swimming pool showing undulating wave wall

6

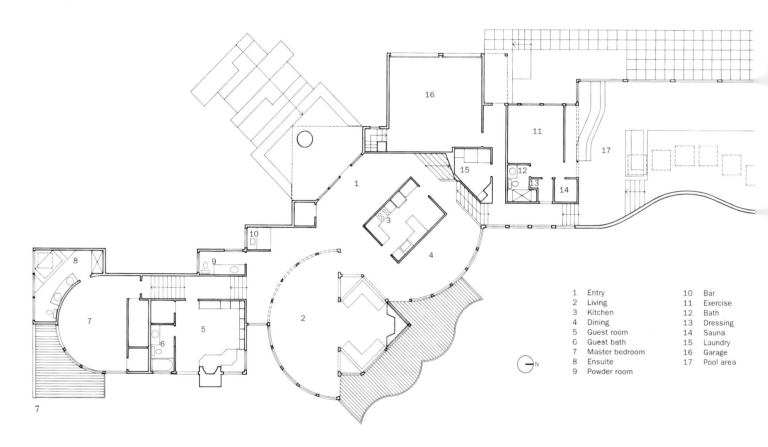

1	Entry	10	Bar
2	Living	11	Exercise
3	Kitchen	12	Bath
4	Dining	13	Dressing
5	Guest room	14	Sauna
6	Guest bath	15	Laundry
7	Master bedroom	16	Garage
8	Ensuite	17	Pool area
9	Powder room		

7

8

9

10

11

12

13

14

15

13   Living room fireplace
14   Living room steps
15   Living room toward fireplace
16   Kitchen
17   Master bedroom
18   Circular wall in the living room

16

17

18

New Vernon House

Design/Completion 1986/1987
New Vernon, New Jersey
7,120 square feet (site area: 2 acres)
Wood frame
Exterior insulating finish system, rubber roofs, sheetrock interior finish,
hardwood and carpet floors

The wooded site slopes gently to the south, and the first view of the house is from a winding downhill drive. The architects planned the first glimpse of the house to include a bowed front with a curved colonnade and covered entrance. For emphasis, the facade is banded with two colors.

A few steps lead down from the entrance to an atrium, which is the focus of the house. A continuous skylight illuminates the walls of this room, and details have been curved and shaped to provide vistas of surrounding spaces. From the center front hall, a sculptural staircase leads to second floor bedrooms.

1   Exterior
2   Window detail
3   Exterior
4   Ground floor plan
5   Living room
6   View to exterior
7   Ceiling of living room

1

2

3

216

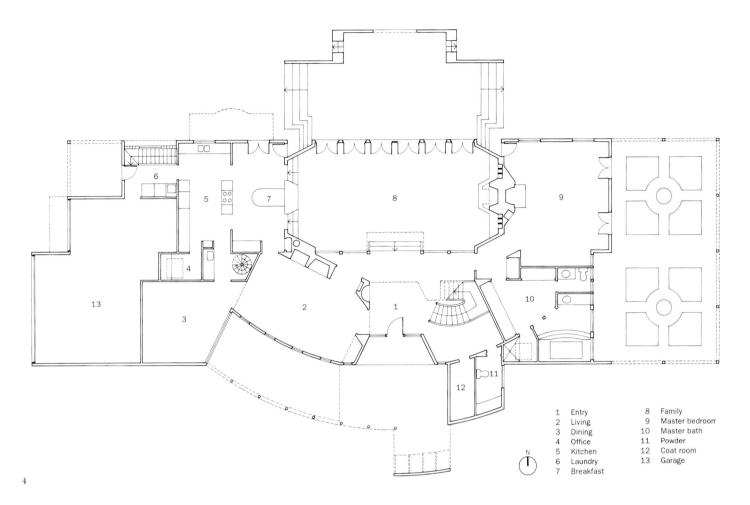

4

1 Entry
2 Living
3 Dining
4 Office
5 Kitchen
6 Laundry
7 Breakfast

8 Family
9 Master bedroom
10 Master bath
11 Powder
12 Coat room
13 Garage

N

5

6

7

Quinones/Bieganek House

Design/Completion 1988/1989
East Hampton, New York
Marcello Quinones, Michael Bieganek
Interior Designer: Catherine De Vido
2,435 square feet (site area: 3 acres)
Wood frame
Black stained cedar boards, painted medium-density overlay plywood (exterior), asphalt shingle roofing with copper front accent, painted sheetrock (interior), oak flooring

Freshwater wetlands restrictions on this 3-acre woodland property reduced the buildable area to less than one-quarter of an acre. The balance of the property was to be deeded to the Town as an area of scenic beauty, to conserve the natural condition of the land. In addition, the site's high subsurface water table hampered the installation of wells and the septic system and required retaining walls and land contouring.

The design consists of two rectangular blocks, enlivened by a diagonal connection which penetrates the entire composition to form porches and decks at each end. The peaked roofs are set apart by a change in material from shingles to cooper roofing at the center of the composition.

The architect's modular system is dramatized on the outside by means of red-painted panels set against black-stained cedar. Inside the house, the diagonal intersects the rectangular building, providing surprising vistas. A bold round column at the entrance serves as a "hinge" between the entrance and the living areas. The living and dining room furniture, designed by the architects, is in tune with the overall house design.

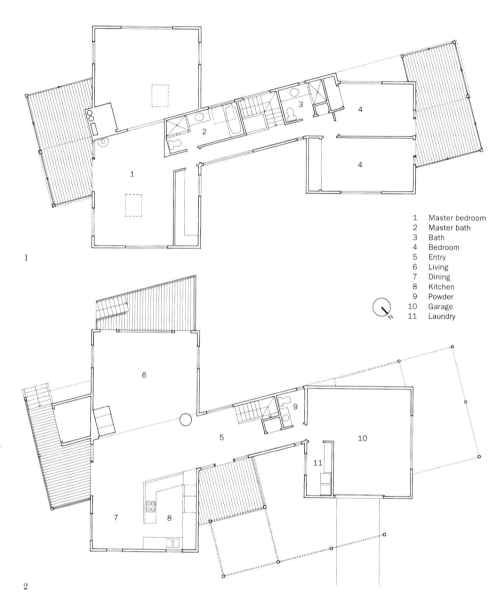

1

2

1 Master bedroom
2 Master bath
3 Bath
4 Bedroom
5 Entry
6 Living
7 Dining
8 Kitchen
9 Powder
10 Garage
11 Laundry

3

4

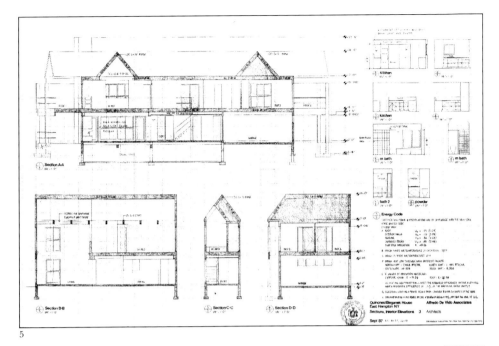

5

6

7

8

1 Second floor plan
2 Ground floor plan
3&4 Exterior views
5 Working drawing
6–8 Exterior views

9&10 Interior views
  11 Bedroom
  12 Architect-designed chest

9

10

11

12

Meadow Way House

Design/Completion 1995/1996
East Hampton, New York
900 square feet addition (site area: 0.25 acre)
Wood frame
Shingles to match existing, painted trim, sheetrock interiors,
hardwood and carpeted floors

Living on a winding village street where
the houses were built in the 1930s and 40s,
it was important to the owners of the
Meadow Way house that their new
addition fit sympathetically and
unobtrusively into the neighborhood.

The architects responded by designing
a new wing using the same materials as
the original house—cedar shingles for the
walls and white trim around the windows
and doors. The shortest side of the
structure was oriented to the street and,
to avoid overwhelming the older house,
the new area was built lower to the
ground.

The transition between the two spaces
is made on the ground floor via a few wide
steps which enter the new living room
at its northern end. At the southern end
of the room, a switch from oak flooring
to brick pavers signals the beginning of
a sun-drenched conservatory full of plants.
The brick continues outside onto a patio,
unifying the indoor and outdoor spaces
and visually extending the space of the
conservatory.

The addition includes a master bedroom
and bath upstairs, as well as a sitting room.

1   Addition
2   Front exterior
3   Living room

1

2

3

House in Bridgehampton

Design/Completion 1973/1974
Bridgehampton, New York
3,000 square feet (site area: 2 acres)
Wood frame on concrete footings
Vertical cedar wood siding; tile, wood and carpeted floors

The site was flat and surrounded on two sides by a curving hedgerow 20 feet high; sun and breezes were to the east and south. The client requested bedrooms for his family of four, a guest room, and a living area and kitchen adjacent to a swimming pool. Detached cabanas near the garage were designed for use with the pool.

Although large, the house was completed on a tight budget per square foot and interior finishes selected with a view to economy. Detailing employs stock windows and conventional framing and finishing techniques.

The design clusters the entry, kitchen, and master bedroom spaces around the major living space. The axis of this space orients furniture around the fireplace at one end and the pool at the other. The other half of the house contains four additional bedrooms, grouping the children's rooms around their own recreation room.

Glass areas are oriented toward the sun and outdoor areas. The entrance and vehicular zone of the site is separated from the living zone by the house itself and a long curving fence which reflects the curving line of the hedgerow.

1

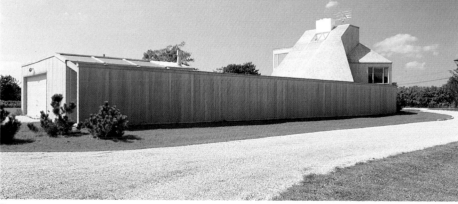

1   Exterior
2   Privacy wall
3   Second floor plan
4   Ground floor plan
5   Kitchen
6&7   Living room

2

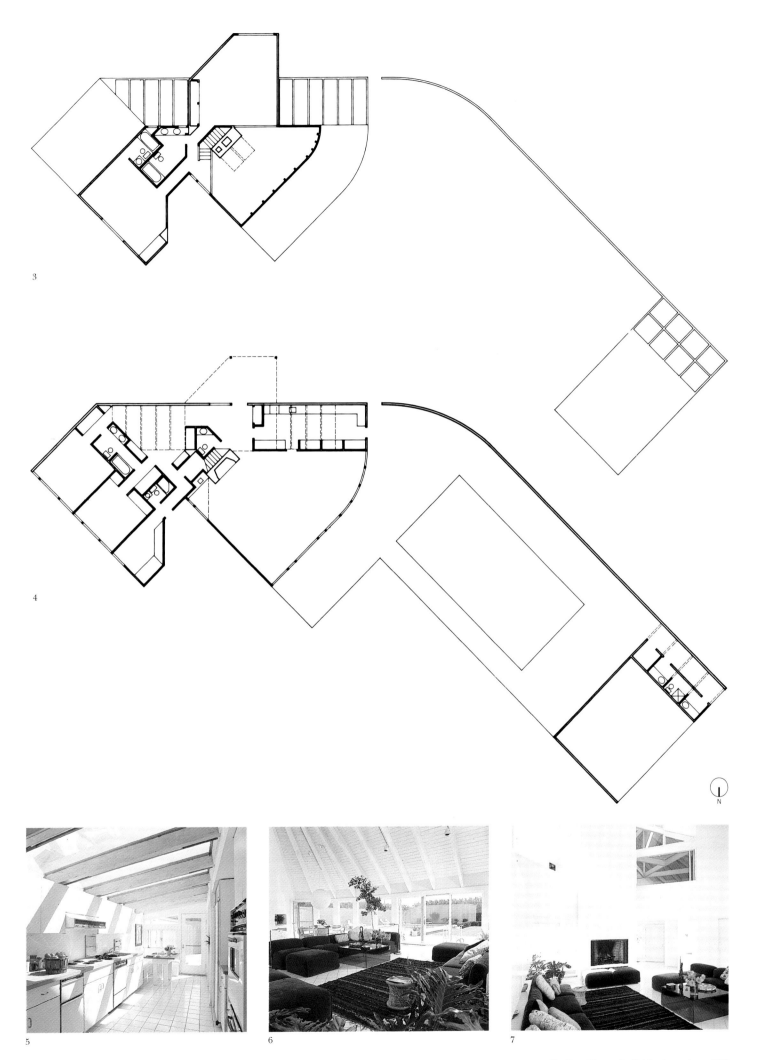

3

4

5   6   7

Haidinger House

Design/Completion 1972/1973
Winhall, Vermont
Mr and Mrs Robert Haidinger
2,000 square feet (site area: 1 acre)
Wood frame, black-stained pine boards in reverse board and batten
pattern (exterior), stained pine boards (interior), carpet and stone floors

In this ski house, the big living room reaches 25 feet at its highest point; the four bedrooms and two bunkrooms sleep 14; and there is a sauna, an "unbundling" room for ski gear with stone floor, and a recreation room. Yet the entire house fits into 2,000 square feet and was built within a tight budget.

The owners, a couple with three children, wanted a simple house requiring little maintenance. The design review board approved this house because of its sturdy character and steeply pitched profile that fits naturally into the mountain setting.

An attractive feature of the house is the way daylight is brought through clerestories into the living room and master bedroom. Carpet and furnishings blend comfortably with the rough Vermont pine of the walls and architect-designed furniture. A broad veranda at the back of the house is used in summer as a sun deck.

1

1   Sketch
2   Exterior
3   Upper level plan
4   Lower level plan
5&6 Exterior views
7&8 Interior views

2

224

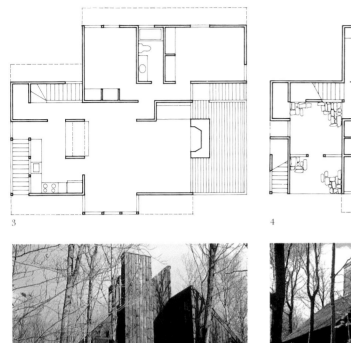

3

4

N

5

6

7

8

Rafferty House

Design/Completion 1972/1973
Vermont
Michael and Mimi Rafferty
2,300 square feet (site area: 1.5 acres)
Wood frame
Reverse board and batten of pine, wood windows, wood shingle roof,
natural cedar wood interior, carpet and wood floors

The owner had acquired a steep site with magnificent views toward distant hills. To take advantage of these natural features, the house was planned on three stepped levels, each provided with generous window areas.

The entrance is at the top level; the living room, master bedroom, and other main spaces take up the middle level; and the lower level contains bunks, a recreation room, and a sauna. To cut down on the heating load, there are clerestories on the southern, uphill side; overhangs protect these openings from the summer sun.

The sequence of levels and rooms was carefully arranged for viewer impact: upon entering at the highest level, one sees only a small section of the view, but as one comes down the staircase into the two-story living room, the full panorama of trees and distant mountains is revealed.

1 Sketch
2&3 Exterior
4 Living room

1

2

3

4

Columbia County House

Design/Completion 1977/1978
Upstate New York
2,000 square feet (site area: 7 acres)
Wood frame, concrete foundations, special drainage below basement due
to hillside location
Vertical cedar siding (exterior), sheetrock (interior), hardwood and
carpeted floors

This hillside house scanning the
Berkshires makes the most of long views
by grouping children's and adults' areas
on either side of a central stair. The stair
rises from the entry and breaks the house
up into five split levels, ensuring privacy
for the family's various activities.

1&2 Exterior views
  3 Lower level plan
  4 Upper level plan

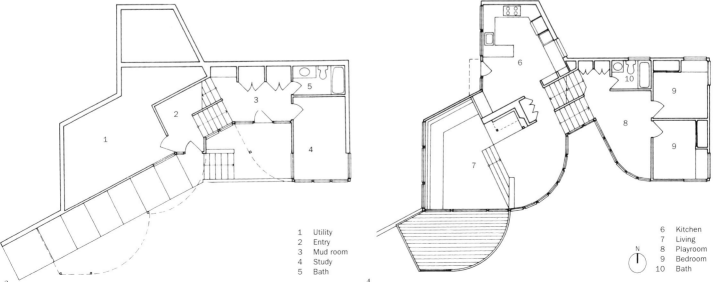

1 Utility
2 Entry
3 Mud room
4 Study
5 Bath

6 Kitchen
7 Living
8 Playroom
9 Bedroom
10 Bath

N

Megerle House

Design/Completion 1978/1979
North Castle, New York
Mr and Mrs Karl Megerle
3,500 square feet (site area: 7 acres)
Wood frame, some steel
Stucco exterior with control joints, glass skylight over garden room, sheetrock interiors, rubber roof

This house combines a number of the owners' specific wishes into a unified scheme. The owners wanted a garden room surrounding an indoor pool as the focus of their house, a view over a pond to the east, and use of solar energy where possible.

Accordingly, the architects arranged a glass roof over the garden room on a diagonal to attain the necessary south orientation; because of the sloping site, the walls were stepped to catch the view. Solar collectors heat the pool water, raising the thermal efficiency of the house and reducing the cost of heating the pool in winter.

Living areas are clustered around the garden room, which includes an enclosed study. Children's bedrooms are in a wing next to a small play/study area and the master bedroom is raised above the living areas for privacy and views.

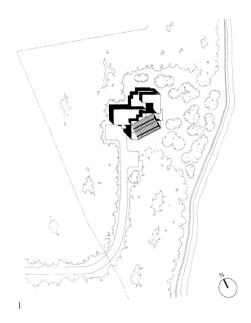

1

2

3

1 Site plan
2 Axonometric
3–6 Exterior views
7 Indoor pool
8 Second floor plan
9 First floor plan

4

5

6

7

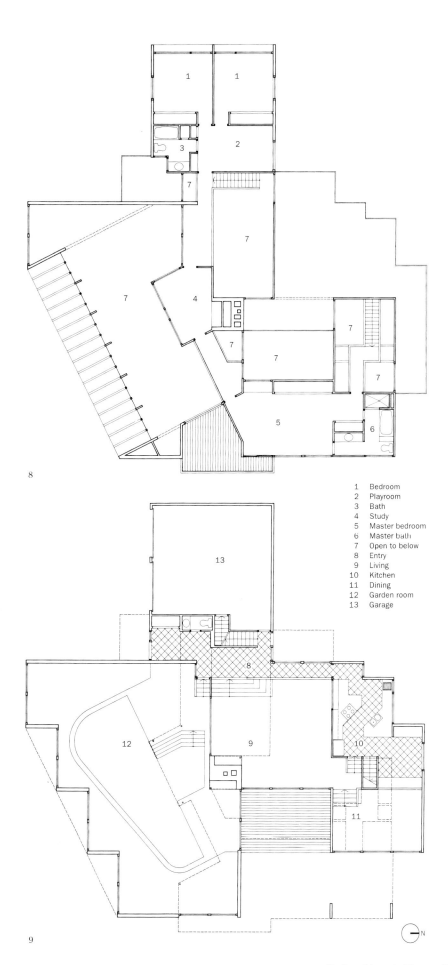

8

1 Bedroom
2 Playroom
3 Bath
4 Study
5 Master bedroom
6 Master bath
7 Open to below
8 Entry
9 Living
10 Kitchen
11 Dining
12 Garden room
13 Garage

9

Moellentine House

Design/Completion 1985/1986
Lakeville, Connecticut
Mr and Mrs Lon Moellentine
4,800 square feet (site area: 5 acres)
Wood frame
White-stained cedar boards, pipe rails, flat built-up roof, wood and carpet floors, aluminum thermal windows

This house is located in Lakeville, Connecticut, a small town in the northwestern corner of the state. It is situated on a hilltop with a splendid view of the lake to the south. To focus on this view, we have used curves, setbacks, and large glass areas.

The glass areas are stepped back so sunlight can penetrate into rooms on the north side of the building and to allow these rooms to benefit from the view as well. The south-facing glass gives the added advantage of solar gain, which is retained by the slate floors in the living area. The windows are arranged in a grid pattern.

The main living area is on the same level as the entrance, on the uphill side of the house. Due to the steep slope, this scheme enabled a lower level to be planned for guest rooms and recreation areas. The master bedroom suite and a studio are located above these spaces.

The kitchen, adjacent to the living area, is finished in imported Italian black lacquer. Whimsical tiles in the studio and baths are also Italian.

1

1&2   Exterior
  3   Interior

2

3

Peters House

Design/Completion 1978/1979
North Castle, New York
3,000 square feet (site area: 2 acres)
Wood frame
Stained cedar boards (exterior); painted sheetrock (interior); wood, tile, and carpet floors; natural hardwood cabinetry

The design program called for a large number of bedrooms for the owners and their five children. The steep and rocky site was almost unbuildable and the large floor area required had to be compressed onto a small outcropping, resulting in a compact plan which rises vertically.

The heart of the house is the family/ dining/kitchen area which opens to large decks. Overlooking this area, but separated acoustically by fixed sheets of glass, is a second living area, designed for quiet activities. This device is also used with some of the bedrooms, to permit visual interpenetration of the room and the flow of light from one to the other.

The master bedroom is on the highest level, with an adjacent study and deck. It enjoys a fine view of the distant New York skyline. Family dining is off the kitchen/family room in a greenhouse enclosure.

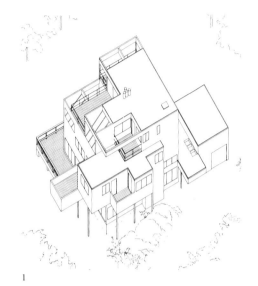

1   Axonometric
2&3   Interior views
4   Exterior

3

4

Turchin House

Design/Completion 1991/1992
East Hampton, New York
Martin and Cheryl Turchin
7,250 square feet (site area: 3 acres)
Wood frame.
Exterior insulating finish system; tile trim; wood windows; sheetrock
interior; tile, carpet, and hardwood floors

This hillside house was designed to
capture views to the east and south,
provide shade around well-defined courts,
and act as a backdrop for the owner's
collection of art and objects.

The north court is the entrance and
provides shelter from ocean winds. The
south court is larger and is surrounded
by latticed porticoes which provide sun
control around the pool. Fountains
enliven the composition.

From the entry, an axial view of the south
court is seen. In the living/dining area,
a three-layer window system controls the
temperature. Adjacent to the kitchen,
a screened porch that commands a fine
view acts as an outdoor dining room.
The master bedroom is quietly situated,
looking east and south over the court.
Other bedrooms are located on the
second floor.

Materials, mainly tile, stone, wood, and
Dryvit, are neutral in color and detailed
in execution.

1

2

3

4

1   Exterior
2   Trellis
3   Living room
4   Exterior
5   Exterior seating area

5

Senkirk House

Design/Completion 1996/1997
East Hampton, New York
Ronald L. Senkirk
3,500 square feet (site area: 2 acres)
Wood frame, concrete foundation
Exterior insulation system, wood shingle roof, wood fixed and casement windows, painted and papered sheetrock interior walls and ceilings, hardwood floors

The client requested a large central living area in proximity to a media room and dining room. The architects responded with a central building mass that accommodates an entry, a living room, and a dining room. The volume of space here is large.

A pair of stairs at the entry lead to two separate bedrooms. A third bedroom, placed above the living room and overlooking a rear garden, can be reached by either set of stairs.

The exterior of the building is clad in an insulating system pierced with paned openings to maintain the planar quality of the house. Porches define the front and rear access of the symmetrical composition. A covered walkway connects the house to a separate garage.

1

2

3

4

5

6

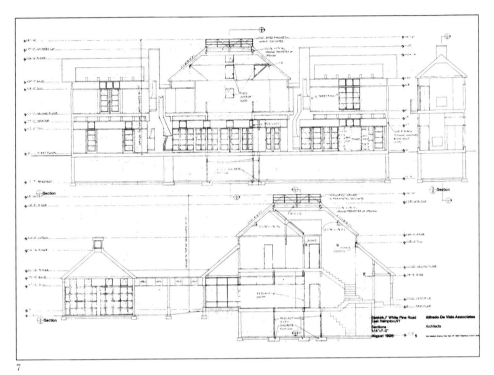

7

8

9

10

11

12

1   Front
2   Rear porch
3   Front porch
4   Side
5   Rear
6   Connection to garage
7   Working drawing
8   View from second floor
9   View from rear porch
10 Living room
11 Living room fireplace
12 Living room

Architect's House and Office, 412 East 85th Street

Design/Completion 1996/1998
New York, New York
Alfredo and Catherine De Vido
5,000 square feet (site area: 2,200 square feet)
Wood frame, existing brick and stone foundation
Horizontal cedar boards (painted); wood double-hung windows; existing
wood structure resheathed with wood; new wood and tile floors; existing
plaster resurfaced or repainted; new wood trim, detail, and cabinetry.

In the process of looking for a new office and dwelling, the architect came across a mid-1800s clapboard house in need of major renovation. The decision was made to purchase the house and divide it into an office, a dwelling, and a rental apartment. The renovation placed the office on the ground floor, the rental apartment on the top floor, and the living quarters in between.

Exploratory research and probes revealed some of the early aesthetic, such as wider clapboards on the exterior and a continuous front porch, and these were subsequently restored. A decorative cornice in the front hall was stripped to its original plaster finish and the fireplaces in the living room, which needed much restoration work, were given a faux stone finish.

Rooms were redesigned with a proportional system of cabinetry and cornices. The cornices serve as light coves designed to improve room proportions and act as a scribe piece to the uneven ceilings. They are modern in design and proportion but evocative of those that must have existed in the original house. Throughout, the design intent is to evoke and enhance the past rather than emulate it. The mechanical and functional elements of the house were completely redesigned.

1

1   Street facade
2   Stair hall
3   Living room
4   Stair at second floor
5&6   Living room

2

3

4

5

6

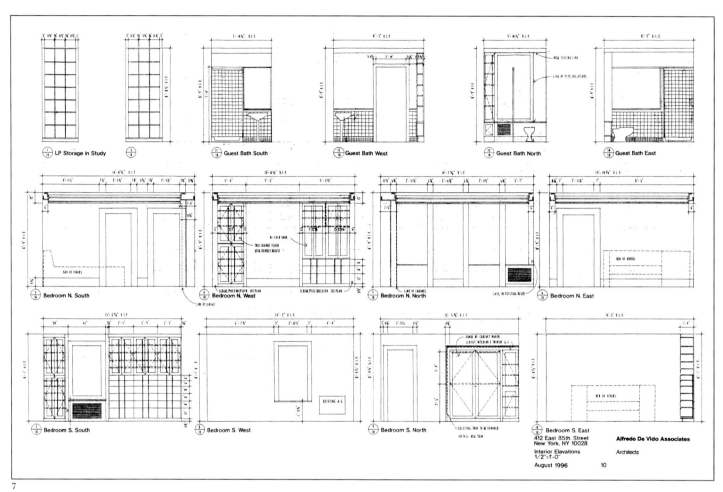

7

8

9

7   Working drawings showing cabinetry
8   Study
9   Storage room
10 Living room
11 Living room storage unit
12 Kitchen
13 Living room storage unit

10

11

12

13

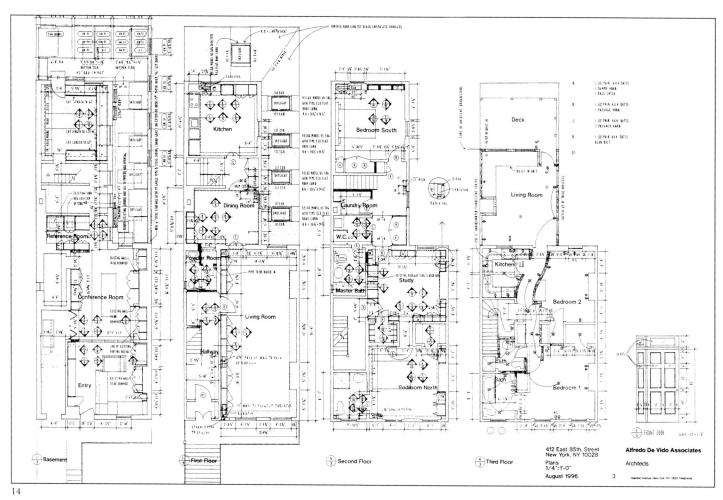

Kitchen

Dining Room

Reference Room

Powder Room

Conference Room

Living Room

Hallway

Entry

Bedroom South

Laundry Room

W.C.

Study

Master Bath

Bedroom North

Deck

Living Room

Kitchen

Bedroom 2

Bath

Bath

Bedroom 1

FRONT DOOR

412 East 85th. Street
New York, NY 10028

Plans
1/4"=1'-0"

August 1996

Alfredo De Vido Associates

Architects

3   Madison Avenue New York, NY 10021 Telephone

Basement   First Floor   Second Floor   Third Floor

14

15

16

14   Plans
15   Master bedroom
16   Guest bathroom
17   Office
18   Back stair detail
19&20   Study

17

18

19

20

Furniture and Lighting

The architect has designed furniture and lighting fixtures as an adjunct to some projects. Custom furniture can be competitive with high-quality stock or designed pieces if the local cabinetmaker is enlisted as part of the team.

Comfort is mandatory when designing chairs. The architect recommends a mock-up be made and tested by the client before fabrication of multiple units.

Storage is routinely designed by the architect and customized from within to fit the clients' needs. Free-standing pieces are sometimes more appropriate and can fit distinctively into the design scheme, as in Quinones/Bieganek House (pages 244 and 245).

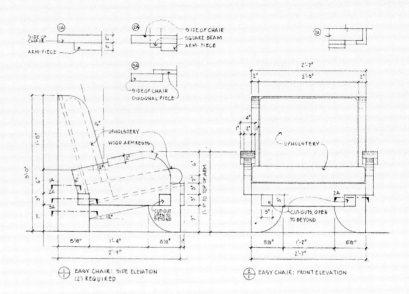

EASY CHAIR: SIDE ELEVATION
(2) REQUIRED

EASY CHAIR: FRONT ELEVATION

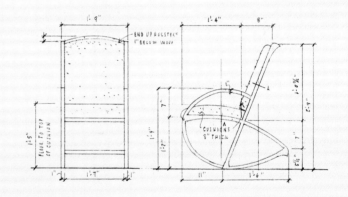

PLAN
SCALE 1/2"=1'-0"

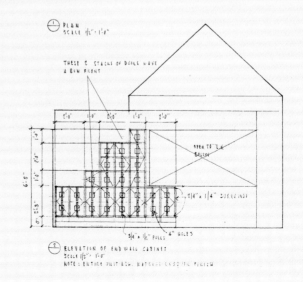

ELEVATION OF END WALL CABINET
SCALE 1/2"=1'-0"
NOTE: ENTIRE UNIT TO MATCH CABINET FINISH

1

2

3

4

5

6

7

Frocht House
1   Master bed with canopy
2   Wall lighting in master bedroom

Walderman Apartment
3   Coffee table
4   Bureau
5   Dining table and chairs

McConomy House
6&7   Chair and occasional table

2 White Pine Road

8 Living room tables, and lamps on walls
   (from industrial components)

9 Bedroom chest, TV cabinet, and armoire

Frocht House

10 Living room chairs, occasional table, and lights
    (stock fixture on mounting blocks in color)

Quinones/Bieganek

11 Chaise lounge in bedroom

14 Free-standing storage unit

Cafe Word of Mouth

12 Dining chairs, tables, and overhead lights

Levy House

13 Built-in sofa

Wright House

15 Living room chairs and occasional tables

8

9

10

11

12

13

14

15

16

17

18

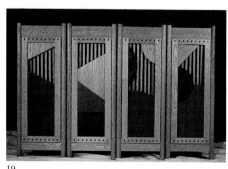

19

20

21

22

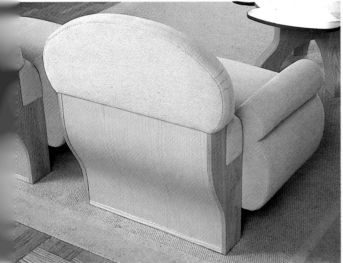

23

24

25

26

27

Levy House

16 Interior bay window

17 TV cabinet

20 Corner display unit

Chapel of Mt St Dominic

18 Altar, altar chair, processional cross, candlesticks, lecterns, baptismal font, tabernacle

Frocht House

19 Back detail of dining chairs

21 Living room chairs and occasional table

Walderman Apartment

22 Sofa

23 Back detail of easy chairs

Quinones/Bieganek

24 Bed and canopy, storage column, and easy chair

Coppola Addition

25 Dining room table, chairs, and sideboard

Wright House

26 Entrance display cabinet

27 Living room chair

Firm Profile

Biography

Alfredo De Vido received a Bachelor of Architecture degree from Carnegie Mellon University in 1954. He was awarded the American Institute of Architects Prize and the Pennsylvania Society of Architects Award for his school work. He went on to receive a Master of Fine Arts in Architecture degree from Princeton University in 1956.

Mr De Vido served for three years in Japan in the US Navy Civil Engineers Corp. ("Seabees"). His work for the Navy included the design and construction of government facilities and buildings, and the design of seven houses for senior officers at US Naval Air Station Atsugi. For this work he was commended by the regional Japanese government.

Following naval service, Mr De Vido attended the Royal Academy of Fine Arts in Copenhagen, where he received a Diploma in Town Planning. During this time he worked in various town planning offices, including that of Professor Peter Bredsdorff.

After Denmark and subsequent travel, Mr De Vido worked in Italy in the offices of The Architects Collaborative (Gropius) and Luigi Moretti.

Upon his return to the USA, Mr De Vido worked with Marcel Breuer and Ernest J. Kump, and as the associate and partner of John H. MacFadyen and Edward F. Knowles, before founding the firm of Alfredo De Vido Architects in 1968.

Mr De Vido's career has continued with the design and construction of houses and housing developments, and also of theaters, which have become an increasingly important part of the firm's work. Other architectural projects have included retail shops, offices, historic renovations, and parks. Working on a steady flow of single-family houses has led him to develop modular systems as an aid to design innovation and construction.

Mr De Vido is a member of the American Institute of Architects College of Fellows. He has served as a member and chairman of AIA committees and design award juries and has lectured and taught at architectural schools throughout the USA and Canada.

Selected Awards

Alfredo De Vido Architects has received numerous design awards from the New York State Association of Architects and the New York City Chapter of the AIA, an American Institute of Architects National Honor Award for Achievement in Design, awards from Connecticut and Long Island Chapters of the AIA, and recognition by *Architectural Record* magazine for excellence in house design.

Selected Bibliography

The work of Alfredo De Vido has been published widely. Books which feature his work include the following:

10 Houses: Alfredo De Vido Architects. Gloucester, Massachusetts: Rockport Publishers, 1998.

Colquhoun, Ian & Peter G. Fauset. *Housing Design.* London: Longman, 1991.

Faulkner, Ray & Sarah Faulkner. *Inside Today's Home.* New York: Holt, 1975.

Goldberger, Paul. *Houses of the Hamptons.* New York: Knopf, 1986.

Kidder-Smith, G.E. *The Architecture of the United States.* New York: MOMA/Anchor, 1981.

Pile, John. *Color in Interior Design.* New York: McGraw-Hill, 1997.

Stern, Robert A (with Clay Lancaster). *East Hampton's Heritage: An Illustrated Architectural Record.* New York: Norton, 1982.

Stimpson, Miriam F. *A Field Guide to Landmarks of Modern Architecture in the United States.* New York: Prentice-Hall, 1985.

Thompson, Elisabeth Kendall. *Recycling Buildings: Renovations, Remodelings, Restorations, and Reuses.* New York: McGraw-Hill, 1977.

Willensky, Elliot & Norval White. *The AIA Guide to New York City.* New York: Harcourt Brace, 1988.

Additionally, his work has been published in many journals, including *Architectural Record, Architecture, House Beautiful, House and Garden, Ville Giardini, Baumeister, Architecture + Urbanism,* as well as in *The New York Times.*

Alfredo De Vido is the author of *Designing Your Client's House* (Whitney, 1983); *Innovative Management Techniques for Architectural Design and Construction* (Whitney, 1984); and *House Design: Art and Practice* (Wiley, 1996).

Acknowledgments

The projects in this book have been made possible through the work and participation of many talented and enthusiastic people. Early theater projects were done in partnership with John H. MacFadyen and Edward F. Knowles.

Architecture requires patronage, and our clients have been some of our most energetic and inspirational supporters. We also want to acknowledge our assistants and consultants who have contributed to these projects, and the contractors and subcontractors who have been a great source of advice and expertise.

Since our work frequently attempts complex spatial compositions, our collaborations with structural engineers have been especially important. Many thanks to Charles Thornton and Paul Gossen for their imagination and support.

The superior quality of the photographs in this book is due to the work of a number of photographers with whom we have worked, notably Norman McGrath, Ezra Stoller, Paul Warchol, Bill Maris, and Fred Charles, among others.

Paul Latham and Alessina Brooks of The Images Publishing Group have made this book possible, with Rod Gilbert overseeing the layout.

Special thanks go to my wife and colleague, Catherine De Vido.

Index

1 White Pine Road 130

3 White Pine Road 128

54 Willow Street 190

70 East 10th Street, New York 46

222 Columbia Heights 186

Aksen House 160

Allendale Park Modular Industrial
Buildings 54

Allen-Stevenson School 84

Apartment, 61 East 86 Street 194

Architect's House and Office,
412 East 85th Street 236

Architect's Office, 699 Madison Avenue 50

Berk of Burlington Arcade 21

Berkowitz Addition/Renovation 145

Boyle House 159

Brooklyn Academy of Music Renovation 72

Built-for-Sale House 136

Butler/Schnur House, 10 White Pine Road
172

Cafe Word of Mouth 26

Catherine Atzen Day Spa 24

Chapel of Mt St Dominic 86

Church's English Shoes 20

Cohalan House 198

Columbia County House 227

Community Church of Astoria 90

Concept House 166

David Alan House 161

De Vido House 122

Diller-Quaile School of Music 82

Drake House 210

Duffy House 121

Evidence Vehicle Facility 57

Farese House 116

Ferguson House 158

Ford Auditorium (see Henry and Edsel
Ford Auditorium Renovation)

Fried House 138

Frocht House 174

Furniture 243

Garraty House 106

Goodman House 137

Greenbriar 148

Gropp House 167

Haidinger House 224

Hammer House 134

Henry and Edsel Ford Auditorium
Renovation 77

House in Bridgehampton 222

J.J. Lally Chinese Art 36

Jonathan's Landing 192

Kessler House 178

Kleinman House 155

La Chausseria 34

Leader House 150

Lee's Art Shop 18

Lighting 243

Lobby Renovation, 108 East 16th Street 48

Manhattan School of Music Renovation/
Addition 74

Mann Music Center 68

Matthews House 118

McCombe House 147

McConomy Poolhouse, Garden, and
Pavilions 204

Meadow Way House 221

Megerle House 228

Minton House 103

Moellentine House 230

Moore House 96

Morton House 168

Muir, Cornelius, Moore Office
Renovation 45

New Preston House 156

New Vernon House 216

Offices for Import Associates Inc. 44

Peters House 231

Queens Theatre in the Park 78

Quinones/Bieganek House 218

Rafferty House 226

Ranch 1 Fast Food Restaurant 42

Ross House 127

Rothschild House 170

Royale 182

Sametz House 108

Sara House 152

Senkirk House 234

Sheehy House 104

Silver Sands State Park 60

Snow King Inn 140

Staten Island House 200

Stephen Gaynor School 83

Stuarts Restaurant 32

Tess 22

Troa Cho Boutique 40

Trosin House 209

Turchin House 232

Vuolo House 164

WebGenesis 52

Wertheimer House 112

West House 110

Wig Shop 38

Wirth House 100

Wolf Trap Farm Park 64

Word of Mouth 26

Wright House 180

Yang House 146